Responding to Diversity in Schools

Responding to Diversity in Schools provides guidance for education practitioners on how to use an inquiry-based approach in responding to learner diversity. It supports readers in addressing an agenda for change, considering questions such as:

- Who are the learners who are missing out?
- What evidence do we need in order to understand the barriers faced by these learners?
- How can we analyse this evidence in order to find effective ways of moving forward?
- How do we involve others in this process?

Responding to Diversity in Schools sets out to encourage innovation in schools, challenge existing assumptions and practices, and promote critical reflection. The contributing authors explain how to use a wide range of research methods, including visual methods, that can be employed to gather the views of children and young people. In addition, the book provides illustrative examples of innovative approaches to doing research with children, teachers and parents in schools.

Written in a clear, direct style that addresses the types of concerns facing teachers on a daily basis, this book offers both practical guidance on responding to the challenge of diversity and inclusion from an inquiry-based learning perspective, and a range of detailed worked examples from schools. It will support individual practitioners and staff teams working on school development issues, as well as tutors wishing to use inquiry-based approaches within workshops and courses. It will also benefit postgraduate students who are focusing on inclusion, diversity, school development and leadership.

Susie Miles is Programme Director of the M.Ed degree in Inclusive Education at the University of Manchester, UK.

Mel Ainscow is Professor of Education and Co-director of the Centre for Equity in Education at the University of Manchester, UK.

Responding to Diversity in Schools

An inquiry-based approach

Edited by Susie Miles
and Mel Ainscow

Routledge
Taylor & Francis Group

LONDON AND NEW YORK

First edition published 2011
by Routledge
2 Park Square, Milton Park, Abingdon, Oxon, OX14 4RN

Simultaneously published in the USA and Canada
by Routledge
270 Madison Avenue, New York, NY 10016

*Routledge is an imprint of the Taylor & Francis Group, an informa
business*

© 2011 Susie Miles and Mel Ainscow for selection and editorial
material; individual chapters, the contributors

Typeset in Sabon by
Pindar NZ, Auckland, New Zealand
Printed and bound in Great Britain by
CPI Antony Rowe, Chippenham, Wiltshire

British Library Cataloguing in Publication Data
A catalogue record for this book is available from the British
Library

Library of Congress Cataloging-in-Publication Data
Responding to diversity in schools: an inquiry based approach /
edited by Susie Miles and Mel Ainscow.
        p. cm.
    Includes bibliographical references.
    1. Multicultural education. 2. Inclusive education. 3. Teachers—
Training of. I. Miles, Susie. II. Ainscow, Mel.
    LC1099.3.R4854 2011
    370.117—dc22   2010010226

ISBN13: 978-0-415-57576-8 (hbk)
ISBN13: 978-0-415-57577-5 (pbk)
ISBN13: 978-0-203-84340-6 (ebk)

Contents

Contributors

Editors

Mel Ainscow is Professor of Education and Co-director of the Centre for Equity in Education at the University of Manchester. He is also the government's Chief Adviser for the Greater Manchester Challenge, a £50 million initiative to improve educational outcomes for all young people in the region. Previously a head teacher, local education authority inspector and lecturer at the University of Cambridge, Mel's work attempts to explore connections between inclusion, teacher development and school improvement.

Susie Miles has been Programme Director of the M.Ed degree in Inclusive Education at the University of Manchester since 2005. She began her career as a teacher of deaf children, and went on to become Save the Children UK's Regional Disability Adviser for Southern Africa, where she was centrally involved in developing national policies and innovative programmes in education and disability in seven countries in the region. In 1997, she played a key role in setting up the Enabling Education Network (EENET), which has become a unique international resource on inclusive education. Her research explores ways of sharing practice in education, and inclusive education in particular, between different cultural contexts – with a particular focus on developing country contexts.

Contributing authors

Pamela Aspin is a qualified teacher with seven years' experience in the classroom, including one year spent teaching Grade 3 in Minnesota, USA, as part of the Fulbright Teacher Exchange Program. She later joined a local education authority support service as a behaviour advisory teacher and is currently working as part of a multidisciplinary team in the Targeted Mental Health in Schools programme (TaMHS), which is funded by the Department for Education (formerly Department for Children, Schools and Families). She graduated in 2009 from the University of Manchester with a Master's degree in Special and Inclusive Education.

Rosanne Brinkhuis completed her Master's degree in Education in the Netherlands, and wrote her final thesis on primary school councils and their influence on the perceived autonomy of pupils. She is now an educational adviser at the INHolland University of Applied Sciences, where she works on multicultural integration and develops educational programmes for students with above average results, in addition to their regular curriculum.

Sarah Butson currently works in primary care with the Élisabeth Bruyère Research Institute in Ottawa, Canada. She holds an MSc in Educational Research from the University of Manchester and formerly worked as a teacher and special needs coordinator for a private high school in Toronto. In both roles she has conducted an array of qualitative and quantitative research projects, and has a special interest in equity and inclusion, as well as cognitive psychology.

Felicity Chambers worked as a secondary mathematics teacher for children in public care and those excluded from mainstream education. She went on to study a Master's in Statistics and a Master's in Educational Research, and is currently doing doctoral research, following the transition of Year 6 students who have been identified as having social, emotional and behavioural difficulties into secondary education.

Annita Eliadou holds a Bachelor's degree in Human Behavioural Biology from the University of Toronto, Canada, and has completed the post-graduate degrees of M.Ed in Special and Inclusive Education and MSc in Educational Research at the University of Manchester. She is currently carrying out fieldwork for her PhD in her home country of Cyprus, and her research interests lie in ethnic, religious and linguistically diverse student populations in different educational settings. She has also conducted research on behalf of the Centre for Equity in Education while undertaking her doctoral studies at the University of Manchester.

Emma Lindley did her first degree in English, and worked in education and arts administration before taking a Master's degree in Educational Research. She is now in the final stages of her PhD, investigating approaches to teaching adolescents about mental illness.

Maria Machalepis has a Master's degree in Inclusive Education from the University of Manchester, and has research interests in participatory photography and issues affecting parents for students identified as having special education needs in Cyprus. She has recently returned from Australia where she worked with children who are on the autistic spectrum.

Debra Martin is currently working as a teacher in a pupil referral unit in the UK, while studying part time for a Master's degree in Inclusive Education. She has a particular interest in the specific and changing needs of young people who are outside mainstream education.

Myriam Mojica Martínez has an MA in Special Educational Needs from the University of Leeds and is currently a PhD student in the School of Education at the University of Manchester. Her main area of research is the inclusion of children with autism in her home country of Mexico.

Clare Millington has a first degree in Geology and was a science teacher in secondary and further education for eight years. Having discovered that some of the most exciting teaching and learning occurs outside the classroom, she then went on to run a successful business in environmental education for twelve years. Her route into special education came through her efforts to understand the options facing her disabled twins in the English education system, and this has led her to return to the indoor classroom to work on the inclusion of children with complex needs in mainstream schools, while studying for a Master's degree in Inclusive Education at the University of Manchester.

Michele Moore has over twenty years' experience as a teacher and school senior manager, and worked as a local authority adviser in developing and managing a local authority-wide inclusion strategy. In this role, she collaborated with the University of Manchester in developing partnership work between students, teachers and the University, while completing a Master's in Special and Inclusive Education. She has recently had a coordinating role within the gifted and talented strand of the City Challenge programme, where her primary aim was to increase progression to the most competitive courses in universities for disadvantaged and vulnerable students. Currently she is Programme Leader for Special Educational Needs and Disability at the Training and Development Agency (TDA).

A disruptive and disaffected pupil at school, **Zoe O'Riordan** failed her A-levels and spent the next nine years travelling and in dead-end jobs. She drifted into residential care work in a school for boys with emotional and behavioural difficulties. Unhappy with the way the boys were treated, she decided to study 'how it should be done' and is currently an Economic and Social Research Council (ESRC)-funded PhD student at the University of Manchester, researching the transitional experiences of school leavers with social, emotional and behavioural difficulties.

Harriet Rowley is a trained teacher and is currently studying for her PhD at the University of Manchester. She has taught and conducted research in a range of environments, including special schools in the UK, Nepal and India. Her research interests are concerned with issues of equity in schools, particularly in relation to disadvantaged neighbourhoods in UK urban contexts.

Formerly a lecturer in Child Development at the University of Delhi, **Abha Sandill** is currently a doctoral student at the University of Manchester, and is researching the role of school leadership in responding to diversity in schools in India. She has worked on several research projects in India, including the inclusion of children with disabilities in regular schools at a national level, and the impact of early childhood care services on children living in disadvantaged urban settings.

Hannah Scott is interested in student diversity in further education, with a particular focus on multiple intelligences theory and its applications, the learning experiences of students described to have learning difficulties and educators' perceptions of them. She is a qualified further education tutor with a BA in Learning Disability Studies and an MSc in Educational Research. She is currently writing up her PhD research, which was ESRC funded.

Linda Verhaar recently completed an MPhil in Educational Sciences (Developmental Disorders) in the Netherlands. She wrote her final thesis on the relationship between medication and drug abuse in children with attention deficit and hyperactivity disorders. She is currently working with children with developmental disorders and has research interests in children who have special needs.

Malcolm Williams is currently employed as the Curriculum Manager in a special school for children with social, emotional and behavioural difficulties. He spent the first four years of his working life in the Merchant Navy and then moved to the British Army where he completed twelve years' service. He has a degree in Social Anthropology and is in the final stages of completing a Master's degree in Inclusive Education at the University of Manchester.

Preface

The ideas presented in this book have evolved from a programme of research carried out by colleagues in the School of Education at the University of Manchester over the last 15 years. This research has focused on one of the major issues facing policy makers and practitioners – that of developing schools that can provide an effective education for all children and young people, whatever their characteristics or circumstances.

A distinctive feature of the research is that it has been carried out *with* schools, rather than *on* them. In this way, we have tried to ensure that the focus is on authentic issues facing the field, and that any proposals that emerge are relevant and feasible within the day-to-day realities of school life. Most of this earlier research has already been published in forms that are relevant to both academic and professional audiences. References as to how this material can be accessed are provided in the chapters.

What the book adds to this literature are rich accounts of attempts to make use of the lessons of the research in a varied range of contexts. In this way, we set out to offer guidance to practitioners as to how to use an inquiry-based approach to learner diversity in schools.

We believe that *Responding to Diversity* is relevant to a wide audience, including individual practitioners and staff teams working on school development issues; postgraduate students who are focusing on inclusion, diversity, school development and leadership; teachers embarking upon Master's degrees; and tutors wishing to use inquiry-based approaches within workshops and courses.

Given the history of the book, it is hardly surprising that many colleagues have influenced the ideas we present. Many of these are teachers in the schools we have collaborated with – here in the United Kingdom and in countries as diverse as Australia, Brazil, China, Hong Kong, Italy, Portugal, Romania, Spain and Zambia. In thanking them all anonymously, we celebrate their professional commitment in being so willing to join us on our learning journey.

We are also conscious of how, over many years, our ideas have been influenced by colleagues in Manchester and elsewhere. In particular, we want to acknowledge the contributions of Tony Booth, Suzanne Carrington, Paul Clarke, Jo Deppler, Alan Dyson, Peter Farrell, Michael Fielding, Chris Forlin, Sam Fox, Sue Goldrick, David Hargreaves, Susan Hart, David Hopkins, Andy Howes, Ian Kaplan, Judy Kugelmass, Kiki Messiou, Julianne Moss, Sharon Moss, Judy Sebba, Tom Skrtic, Roger Slee, Dave Tweddle and Mel West. Finally, we must thank Michele Moore who made a major contribution in helping to set up many of the school-based projects reported in the book.

Susie Miles and Mel Ainscow
University of Manchester
February 2010

Introduction

Learning about diversity

Mel Ainscow and Susie Miles

> This introductory chapter outlines the rationale for using co-operative, evidence-based approaches of the sort illustrated in the subsequent three parts of the book. In so doing, it draws on the experiences and findings of some 15 years of research carried out by staff and students at the University of Manchester. This research has shown how processes of social learning, stimulated by inquiry, can foster a greater capacity for responding to learner diversity. Collaboration and the use of evidence as a means of stimulating experimentation are seen as key strategies for moving such processes in a more inclusive direction.

Recent years have seen extensive efforts in many countries to ensure that all children and young people receive an effective form of education. These experiences have made it increasingly apparent that traditional forms of schooling are no longer adequate for the challenges of the twenty-first century. Faced with the presence of students whose cultural experiences and languages may be different from their own, and many others who may experience barriers to their learning within conventional arrangements, education practitioners have to think about how they should respond.

In the income-poor countries of the so-called developing world, the Education for All movement has sought to ensure that all children receive at least six years of basic education. It is currently estimated that at least 72 million children worldwide do not attend school at all and a much larger number drop out of education (UNESCO, 2010). However, a preoccupation with ensuring access to education has sometimes led to a decline in the quality of provision.

Meanwhile, in the wealthier countries of the 'developed' industrialised world, despite the resources that are available, many young people leave school with no worthwhile qualifications, while others are placed in various forms of special provision away from mainstream educational experiences, and some simply choose to drop out since the lessons seem irrelevant to their lives (Ainscow and Miles, 2008).

So, what kinds of practices might help schools reach out to all of their learners? How can such practices be developed? How can we ensure that such practices are of high quality, inclusive in the broadest possible sense and respectful of diversity? How can learners themselves play a greater role in improving the educational experience for all? What methods of inquiry need to be developed to promote more relevant forms of research? And what role can school-based inquiry play in stimulating and even initiating change?

These are some of the questions this book sets out to address. In this introductory chapter we summarise the overall rationale for the approach we are recommending, drawing on research carried out at the University of Manchester.

Responding to learner diversity

Traditionally, education systems have responded to diverse groups of learners through the establishment of various forms of separate provision. However, the approaches developed as part of what is now often referred to as 'special needs education' have, despite good intentions, continued to create barriers to progress as schools have been encouraged to adopt them (Ainscow, 1998; Slee, 1996). Furthermore, researchers who have reviewed the evidence for using specialised methods for particular categories of students conclude that there is little support for a separate special needs pedagogy (Davis and Florian, 2004; Lewis and Norwich, 2005). And our own research suggests that the preoccupation with individualised responses that have been the feature of the field of special education also tend to deflect attention away from the creation of practices that can reach out to all learners within a class and the establishment of school conditions that will encourage such developments (Ainscow, 1997, 1999, 2007).

This may help to explain why efforts to respond to learner diversity that are dependent upon the importing of practices from special education tend to foster the development of new, more subtle forms of segregation, albeit within mainstream settings. So, for example, in England, recent years have seen the introduction of teaching assistants who work alongside class teachers in order to facilitate the presence of those students seen to be vulnerable. Recent research indicates, however, that the presence of such support staff leads to a decline in the extent to which teachers themselves have direct contact with some members of their classes (Blatchford et al., 2009).

Meanwhile, the requirement for individualised education plans has encouraged some school leaders to feel that many more children will require such responses, thus creating budget problems within English local authorities (Ainscow et al., 2000). At the same time, the category 'special educational needs' has become a repository for various groups who suffer discrimination in society, such as those from minority ethnic backgrounds. In this way special education can be a way of hiding discrimination against some groups of students behind an apparently benign label, thus justifying their low attainments and, therefore, their need for separate educational arrangements (Harry, 2007).

The recognition that more inclusive schools will not be achieved by transplanting special education thinking and practice into mainstream contexts points to other possibilities. Many of these relate to the need to move away from the individualised planning frame and towards a perspective that seeks to *personalise* learning through an engagement with the whole class (Ainscow, 1999). In this sense, many ideas about effective teaching are relevant. However, what is particular to an inclusive pedagogy is the way in which teachers conceptualise notions of difference.

As Bartolome (1994) explains, teaching methods are neither devised nor implemented in a vacuum. Design, selection and use of particular teaching approaches and strategies arise from perceptions about learning and learners. In this respect, she argues, even the most pedagogically advanced methods are likely to be ineffective in the hands of those who implicitly or explicitly subscribe to a belief system that regards some students, at best, as disadvantaged and in need of fixing, or, at worst, as deficient and, therefore, beyond fixing.

In thinking about what inclusive practices involve, we also have to be sensitive to the complex nature of teaching. Reflecting on their observations of classroom practices internationally, Stigler and Hiebert (1999, p. 47) suggest that teaching should not be seen as a loose mixture of individual features 'thrown together' by individual practitioners. Rather, they suggest, the practice of a teacher 'works like a machine', with the different elements being interconnected. This means that individual features of practice only make sense in relation to the whole.

Commenting on this formulation, Hargreaves (2003) suggests that teaching practices take the form of 'scripts' that are deeply embedded within teachers, reflecting their life experiences and taken-for-granted assumptions. Consequently, changing one or two features of practice is unlikely to lead to significant improvements in teaching quality, since such superficial changes will leave most elements of the original script undisturbed.

Studying practice

In the United Kingdom, two important studies have looked closely at how practices that respond effectively to learner diversity develop. Significantly, both projects involved researchers working collaboratively with practitioners.

The first study, Learning without Limits, examined ways of teaching that are free from determinist beliefs about ability (Hart, 2003; Hart *et al.*, 2004). The researchers worked closely with a group of teachers who had rejected ideas of fixed ability in order to study their practice. They started from the belief that constraints are placed on children's learning by ability-focused practices that lead young children to define themselves in comparison to their peers.

The researchers argue that the notion of ability as inborn intelligence has come to be seen as a natural way of talking about children that summarises their perceived differences. They go on to suggest that national policies in this country reflect this assumption, making it essential for teachers to compare, categorise and group their students by ability in order to provide appropriate and challenging teaching for all. So, for example, inspectors are expected to check that teaching is differentiated for 'more able', 'average' and 'less able' students. In this context, what is meant by 'ability' is not made explicit, leaving scope for teachers to interpret what is being recommended in ways that suit their own beliefs and views. However, it is noted that the emphasis on target setting and value-added measures of progress leave little scope for teachers who reject the fixed view of measurable ability to hold on to their principles.

Through closely examining the practices and thinking of their teacher partners, the researchers set themselves the task of identifying more just and empowering ways of making sense of learner diversity. In summary, they argue that this would involve teachers treating patterns of achievement and response in a spirit of transformability, seeking to discover what is possible to enhance the capacity of each child in their class to learn, and to create the conditions in which their learning can more fully and effectively flourish.

The researchers explain that the teachers in the study based their practices on a strong conviction that things can change and be changed for the better, recognising that whatever a child's present attainments and characteristics, given the right conditions, their capacity for learning can be enhanced. Approaching their work with this mindset, the teachers involved in the study were seen to analyse gaps between their aspirations for children and what was actually happening during lessons.

The second study, Understanding and Developing Inclusive Practices in Schools, involved members of our Manchester team. Significantly, it also pointed to the importance of inquiry as a stimulus for changing practices. Carried out by a research network that was part of the Economic and Social Research Council's Teaching and Learning Research Programme (Ainscow *et al.*, 2004; Ainscow *et al.*, 2003; Ainscow *et al.*, 2006), the study involved 25 schools in exploring ways of developing inclusion in their own contexts, in collaboration with researchers from three universities. All of this took place within the context of a national policy focused on 'driving up standards' that is generally seen to be unhelpful to the development of inclusive practices.

In broad terms, what was noted in the participating schools was neither the crushing of inclusion by the government's policies for raising standards, nor the rejection of the standards agenda in favour of a radical, inclusive alternative. Certainly, many teachers were concerned about the impact on their work of the standards agenda, and some were committed to views of inclusion which they saw as standing in contradiction to the thrust of national policy. However, in most of the schools, the two agendas remained intertwined. Indeed, the focus on attainment appeared to prompt some teachers to examine issues in relation to the achievements and participation of hitherto marginalised groups that they had previously overlooked. Likewise, the concern with inclusion tended to shape the way the school responded to the imperative to raise standards.

In trying to make sense of the relationship between external imperatives and the processes of change in schools, the study drew on the ideas of Wenger (1998) to reveal how external agendas were mediated by the norms and values of the communities of practice within schools and how they become part of a dialogue whose outcomes can be more, rather than less, inclusive. In this way, the role of national policy emerges from the study in something of a new light. This suggests that schools may be able to engage with what might appear to be unfavourable policy imperatives to produce outcomes that are by no means inevitably non-inclusive.

Interrupting thinking and practice

Together, the findings of these two studies lead to reasons for optimism. They indicate that more inclusive ways of working can emerge from a study of existing practices, set within the internal social dynamics of schools. They also suggest that it is possible to intervene in these dynamics in order to open up new possibilities for moving policy and practice forward.

However, there are significant factors that have to be borne in mind in order to make such interventions effective. In particular, we have to be sensitive to the nature of teaching and the ways in which practice develops. Our research reveals how teachers find it difficult to explain their practices in any detail (Ainscow, 1999). It seems that much of their expertise operates at an intuitive level, as they draw on their previous experiences to address the uncertainties they face in the classroom when members of their classes react in often unpredictable ways. This means that often the most significant decisions are those that are made as the lesson proceeds, through what can be characterised as a process of improvisation that is somewhat analogous to the practice of jazz musicians.

Huberman (1993) used a different set of images to explain the way teachers adjust their established ways of working in an attempt to reach out to members of a class. He compared the work of teachers to that of artisans. An example will illustrate the point he makes. Faced with a leak in a sink, an experienced plumber sets about the task in the certain knowledge that he or she knows how to solve the problem. Since the plumber has fixed many similar leaks before, s/he is confident that one of his usual responses will do the trick. Occasionally, however, the plumber experiences a surprise – their usual repertoire proves to be inadequate. What does the plumber do? Does s/he go on a course? Call for help? Read a manual? More likely they will tinker with the problem pipes until able to invent a solution. So, a new way of working is added to the plumber's repertoire, which, of course, s/he can then take with them to the next leaking sink.

The suggestion is that this is something like the way in which teachers develop their practices. Arguably, the key difference is that teaching is far less predictable than plumbing; so much so that during each lesson there are many 'surprises' to be dealt with and, therefore, far more possibilities for tinkering. For example, there is the student who suddenly wants to tell the teacher about something interesting that happened the previous night; another who asks a question about the subject of the lesson that the teacher has never thought of; and, inevitably, those who lose interest or misbehave in some way. Each of these unexpected events requires an instant decision. Just like the plumber, the teacher has no opportunity to take advice. In this way, new responses are trialled and, where they are found to be of value, added to the teacher's range of usual approaches. Through this form of 'planning in action' teachers learn how to create classroom arrangements that can be more effective in responding to individuals within their classes.

Some years ago, Hart (1996) developed what we see as an important framework that can be used by teachers to probe more rigorously and systematically into classroom situations that have not previously responded to their intuitive responses. Her approach – which she calls 'Innovative Thinking' – is a means of generating new ideas to support children's learning. Using evidence from her partnerships with teachers, Hart demonstrates how this approach can be used to develop the 'thinking-on-the-feet' that teachers carry out within lessons in order to identify further possibilities for responding to learner diversity within a class.

Given these arguments, it is hardly surprising that developments in practice are unlikely to occur without some exposure to what teaching actually looks like when it is being done differently, and exposure to someone who can help teachers understand the difference between what they are doing and what they aspire to do (Elmore *et al.*, 1996). Furthermore, this has to be addressed at the individual level before it can be solved at the organisational level. Indeed, there is evidence that increasing collaboration without specific attention to change at the individual level can simply result in teachers coming together to reinforce existing practices, rather than confronting the difficulties they face in different ways (Lipman, 1997).

At the heart of the processes in schools, where changes in practice do occur, is the development of a common language that colleagues can use to talk to one another and, indeed, to themselves about detailed aspects of their practice (Huberman, 1993). Without such a language teachers find it very difficult to experiment with new possibilities. As we have explained, much of what teachers do during the intensive encounters that occur is carried out at an automatic, intuitive level. Furthermore, there is little time to stop and think.

This is why having the opportunity to see colleagues at work is so crucial to the success of attempts to develop practice. It is through shared experiences that colleagues can help one another to articulate what they currently do and define what they might like to do (Hiebert *et al.*, 2002). It is also the means whereby space is created within which taken-for-granted assumptions about particular groups of learners can be subjected to mutual critique.

Our own research has also shown how engagement with various forms of evidence can help to foster the development of more inclusive ways of working (Ainscow *et al.*, 2003). Specifically, this can help to create space for reappraisal and rethinking by interrupting existing discourses, and by focusing attention on previously overlooked possibilities for moving practice forward. Particularly powerful techniques in this respect involve the use of mutual observation, sometimes through video recordings (Ainscow, 1999, 2003), and evidence collected from students about teaching and learning arrangements within a school using image-based research methods (Ainscow and Kaplan, 2005; Messiou, 2006; Miles and Kaplan, 2005).

Under certain conditions such approaches provide *interruptions* that help to make the familiar unfamiliar in ways that stimulate self-questioning, creativity and action. In so doing, they can sometimes lead to a reframing of perceived problems that, in turn, draws the teacher's attention to new ways of addressing barriers to participation and learning. In many of the inquiries described in this book, outsider student researchers, from a wide variety of backgrounds, have entered unfamiliar contexts and have been remarkably successful in interrupting thinking and practice on a particular issue.

Here our argument is informed by the work of Robinson (1998), who suggests that practices are activities that solve problems in particular situations. This means that to explain a practice is to reveal the problem for which it serves as a solution. So, in working closely with practitioners, we have found that we can make inferences about how school staff have formulated a problem and the assumptions that are involved in the decisions made. We have also observed how initial formulations are sometimes rethought as a result of an engagement with various forms of evidence.

However, this is not in itself a straightforward mechanism for the development of more inclusive practices. A space that is created may be filled according to conflicting agendas. For example, our studies have documented examples of how deeply held beliefs within schools may prevent the experimentation that is necessary in order to foster the development of more inclusive ways of working (Howes and Ainscow, 2006; Ainscow and Kaplan, 2005). This reminds us that it is easy for educational difficulties to be pathologised as difficulties inherent within students. This is true not only of students with disabilities and those defined as 'having special educational needs', but also of those whose socio-economic status, race, language and gender render them problematic to particular teachers in particular schools. Consequently, it is necessary to explore ways of developing the capacity of those within schools to reveal and challenge deeply entrenched deficit views of 'difference', which define certain types of students as 'lacking something' (Trent et al., 1998). This involves being vigilant in scrutinising how deficit assumptions may be influencing perceptions of certain students.

This, in turn, points to the importance of what can be seen as cultural factors. Schein (1985) suggests that cultures are about the deeper levels of basic assumptions and beliefs that are shared by members of an organisation, operating unconsciously to define how they view themselves and their working contexts. The extent to which these values include the acceptance and celebration of difference, and a commitment to offering educational opportunities to all students, coupled with the extent to which they are shared across a school staff, relates to the extent to which students are enabled to participate (Carrington, 1999; Kugelmass, 2001; Rosenholtz, 1989).

Talking about schools, Hargreaves (1995) argues that cultures can be seen as having a reality-defining function, enabling those within an institution to make sense of themselves, their actions and their environment. A current reality-defining function of culture, he suggests, is often a problem-solving function inherited from the past. In this way, today's cultural form created to solve an emergent problem often becomes tomorrow's taken-for-granted recipe for dealing with matters shorn of their novelty.

Changing the norms that exist within a school is difficult, particularly within a context that is faced with so many competing pressures and where practitioners tend to work alone in addressing the problems they face (Fullan, 1991). On the other hand, the presence of children who are not suited to the existing 'menu' of the school can provide some encouragement to explore a more collaborative culture within which teachers support one another in experimenting with new teaching responses. In this way, problem-solving activities gradually become the reality-defining, taken-for-granted functions that are the culture of a school that is more geared towards fostering inclusive ways of working.

The implication of all of this is that becoming more inclusive is a matter of thinking and talking, reviewing and refining practice, and making attempts to develop a more inclusive culture. Such a conceptualisation means that we cannot divorce inclusion from the contexts within which it is developing, nor the social relations that might sustain or limit that development (Dyson, 2006). It is in the complex interplay between individuals, and between groups and individuals, that shared beliefs and values exist, and change. Such beliefs and values are impossible to separate from the relationships in which they are embodied.

Developing inclusive school cultures

There is a body of critical literature highlighting the problems and complexities which emerge when schools attempt to move towards greater inclusion (e.g. Dyson and Millward, 2000; Kugelmass, 2004; Skidmore, 2004). These literatures point to the internal complexities of schools as organisations, and the constraints and contradictions that are generated by the policy environments in which they exist. As such, they usefully problematise the assumptions underlying the more mechanistic approaches to improvement, but stop short of saying how inclusion might actually be developed.

A more promising family of approaches to development starts from the assumption that increasing inclusion is less a set of fixed practices or policies, than a continuous process of deconstructing and reconstructing (Skrtic, 1991; Thomas and Loxley, 2001); what Corbett and Slee (2000) have called the cultural vigilantism of exposing exclusion in all its changing forms and seeking instead to foster an inclusive educational culture.

Where writers have addressed the question of how to develop more inclusive ways of working, they tend to give particular emphasis to characteristics of schools as organisations which stimulate and support this process of interrogation. The American scholar Tom Skrtic argues that schools with what he calls 'adhocratic' configurations are most likely to respond to student diversity in positive and creative ways (1991). Such schools emphasise the pooling of different professional expertise in collaborative processes. Children who cannot easily be educated within the school's established routines are not seen as 'having' problems, but as challenging teachers to re-examine their practices in order to make them more responsive and flexible. Similarly, our own work has outlined 'organisational conditions' – distributed leadership, high levels of staff and student involvement, joint planning, a commitment to inquiry and so on – that promote collaboration and problem-solving amongst staff, and which, therefore, produce more inclusive responses to diversity (Ainscow, 1999).

These themes are further supported by a review of international literature carried out by some of our colleagues that examines the effectiveness of school actions in promoting inclusion (Dyson *et al.*, 2002, 2004). The review concludes that there is a limited, but by no means negligible, body of empirical evidence about the relationship between school action and the participation of all students in the cultures, curricula and communities of their schools. In summary, it suggests that:

- Some schools are characterised by an 'inclusive culture'. Within such schools, there is some degree of consensus amongst adults around values of respect for difference and a commitment to offering all pupils access to learning opportunities. This consensus may not be total and may not necessarily remove all tensions or contradictions in practice. On the other hand, there is likely to be a high level of staff collaboration and joint problem-solving, and similar values and commitments may extend into the student body, and into parent and other community stakeholders in the school.

- The extent to which such inclusive cultures lead directly and unproblematically to enhanced pupil participation is not clear. Some aspects of these cultures, however, can be seen as participatory by definition. For instance, respect for diversity from teachers may itself be understood as a form of participation by children within a school community. Moreover, schools characterised by such cultures are also likely to be characterised by forms of organisation (such as specialist provision being made in the ordinary classroom, rather than by withdrawal) and practice (such as constructivist approaches to teaching and learning) which could be regarded as participatory by definition.
- Schools with inclusive cultures are also likely to be characterised by the presence of leaders who are committed to inclusive values and to a leadership style which encourages a range of individuals to participate in leadership functions. Such schools are also likely to have good links with parents and with their communities.

On the basis of this evidence, the Dyson review team make a number of recommendations for policy and practice. They suggest that attempts to develop inclusive schools should pay attention to the development of inclusive cultures and, particularly, to the building of some degree of consensus around inclusive values within school communities. This leads them to argue that principals and other school leaders should be selected and trained in light of their commitment to inclusive values and their capacity to lead in a participatory manner.

According to the review, there are general principles of school organisation and classroom practice which should be followed, notably: the removal of structural barriers between different groups of students and staff; the dismantling of separate programmes, services and specialisms; and the development of pedagogical approaches (such as constructivist approaches) which enable students to learn together rather than separately. It is also argued that schools should build close relations with parents and communities based on developing a shared commitment to inclusive values.

The implications for practice of such an orientation are illustrated in *The Index for Inclusion* (Booth and Ainscow, 2002). This is a set of review materials that enable schools to draw on the knowledge and views of staff, students, parents/carers and governors about barriers to learning and participation that exist within the existing 'cultures, policies and practices' of schools in order to identify priorities for change. In connecting inclusion with the detail of policy and practice, *The Index* encourages those who use it to build up their own view of inclusion, related to their experience and values, as they work out what policies and practices they wish to promote or discourage. *The Index* can support staff in schools in refining their planning processes, so that these involve wider collaboration and participation and introduce coherence to development (see Rustemier and Booth, 2005). In developing the overall approach recommended in this book, we have found that the indicators and questions provided in *The Index* can be helpful in formulating agendas for school-based inquiry (Booth and Ainscow, 2002).

An inquiry-based approach

What emerges from the evidence we have presented is how social learning processes, stimulated by inquiry within particular contexts, can foster a greater capacity for responding to learner diversity. Collaboration and the use of evidence as a means of stimulating experimentation are seen as key strategies for moving such processes in a more inclusive direction. As Copland (2003) suggests, inquiry can be the 'engine' to enable the distribution of leadership that is needed in order to foster participation, and the 'glue' that can bind a school community together around a common purpose.

All of this has major implications for leadership practice at different levels within schools. In particular, it calls for efforts to encourage coordinated and sustained efforts by staff groups around the idea that changing outcomes for all students is unlikely to be achieved unless there are changes in the behaviours of adults. Consequently, the starting point must be with staff members, in effect, enlarging their capacity to imagine what might be achieved and increasing their sense of accountability for bringing this about. This may also involve tackling taken-for-granted assumptions, most often relating to expectations about certain groups of students, their capabilities and behaviours.

Our argument is based on the central idea that *schools know more than they use* and that the logical starting point for development is with a detailed analysis of existing arrangements. As we have argued, this requires the collection of evidence and an engagement with this information. This allows good practices to be identified and shared, while, at the same time, drawing attention to ways of working that may be creating barriers to the participation and learning of some students. However, as we have stressed, the focus must not only be on practice – it must also address and sometimes challenge the thinking *behind* existing ways of working.

With these arguments in mind, subsequent chapters present accounts of the overall approach to school-based inquiry we have developed over the last ten years or so as part of the M.Ed programme at the University of Manchester. (See the Appendix for an explanation of this programme.) This approach involves experienced practitioners in using evidence to analyse the experience of marginalised groups of learners in order to find effective ways of addressing the barriers they experience.

Each of the accounts presented demonstrates the unique qualities of the context in which the inquiry took place, as well as a combination of innovative and creative methods collaboratively designed to respond to the particular context, and to explore the barriers to learning and participation faced by learners in that context.

In presenting these accounts, our aim is to provide readers with guidance that will encourage and inspire innovation in school contexts, challenge existing assumptions and practices, and promote more self-critical reflection by all involved in the process. We illustrate the way a wide range of research methods can be used by different stakeholders to gather evidence in schools. Although children and young people are at the centre of most of the inquiries, some have also involved teachers, head teachers and parents.

The accounts we provide are all focused on responding to the following overall question: *How can education practitioners respond to learner diversity?* More specifically, they suggest ways of using an inquiry-based approach in relation to the following agenda for change:

- Who are the learners who are missing out in our context?
- What evidence do we need in order to understand the barriers faced by these learners?
- How can we analyse this evidence in order to find effective ways of challenging current practice and promoting more positive responses to learner diversity?
- How do we involve learners in this process in a meaningful way?

The approach we have developed involves three interconnected processes: analysing contexts, making interruptions and creating conversations. Each of these themes is, to some extent, evident in all the chapters. However, for purposes of illustration, we have grouped the chapters into three parts, each relating to their area of emphasis:

1 **Analysing contexts.** As we have explained, our earlier research has thrown light on the way contextual factors create barriers to the participation and learning of some students. Chapters 2–6 explain how evidence of various forms can be used to analyse schools and classrooms in order to identify such barriers and determine resources that can be used to address these difficulties.

2 **Making interruptions.** Progress in addressing diversity requires a more dynamic approach to thinking and practice. Chapters 7–10 illustrate how engaging with evidence can, under certain conditions, create 'interruptions' that challenge the use of language, existing assumptions and established pedagogy, and, in so doing, point towards new ways of conceptualising school policies and practices – ways which had previously been overlooked.

3 **Creating conversations.** Chapters 11–14 illustrate how social learning processes can create opportunities for developing new responses to learner diversity. Creating conversations is a way of 'generating and sharing stories, ideas and experience' (Miles, 2009, p. 24). The accounts also

explore some of the complexities in developing the forms of cooperation involved.

The school-based inquiry and development course which we have developed over the years has involved practitioners from diverse cultural backgrounds with a wide range of professional experiences. Attention has therefore been paid throughout the course to the meaning of diversity in education, and to ensuring that the teaching and learning process is respectful of this diversity. Although the majority of the authors are from the UK, a small number come from other countries, namely Cyprus, India, Mexico and the Netherlands.

At the same time, through our involvement in the Enabling Education Network (EENET is the world's largest information sharing network on inclusive education, focusing particularly on developing countries), we have studied educational experiences in some of the most income-poor countries in the world. This has provided greater insight into the educational challenges facing industrialised countries – by *making the familiar extremely unfamiliar*. Many of the UK-based students have commented on the added value of learning and researching alongside professionals from a wide range of cultural and linguistic backgrounds. This experience has, in turn, brought greater sensitivity to the collaborative inquiry process in school settings, where the learners and their families bring such rich cultural diversity to the learning experience.

However, working collaboratively in groups whose membership is culturally, educationally and linguistically diverse can be either a source of inspiration, or, sometimes, a distraction from the focus of the inquiry. Some of the chapters take an honest look at the difficulties faced in communication (both within the group and with the school) in allocating tasks and responsibilities, and discuss the lessons learned from these difficulties. In this way, the accounts remind us that using the approach to inquiry that we are recommending is not always easy.

References

Ainscow, M. (1997) 'Towards inclusive schooling'. *British Journal of Special Education* 24(1): 3–6.

Ainscow, M. (1998) 'Developing links between special needs and school improvement'. *Support for Learning* 13(2): 70–75.

Ainscow, M. (1999) *Understanding the Development of Inclusive Schools*. London: Falmer.

Ainscow, M. (2007) From special education to effective schools for all: a review of progress so far. In L. Florian (ed.) *The Sage Handbook of Special Education*. London: Sage.

Ainscow, M. and Kaplan, I. (2005) 'Using evidence to encourage inclusive school development: possibilities and challenges'. *Australasian Journal of Special Education* 29(2): 106–116.

Ainscow, M. and Miles, S. (2008) 'Making education for all inclusive: where next?' *Prospects* 38(4): 15–34.

Ainscow, M., Farrell, P. and Tweddle, D. (2000) 'Developing policies for inclusive education: a study of the role of local education authorities'. *International Journal of Inclusive Education* 4(3): 211–229.

Ainscow, M., Howes, A. J., Farrell, P. and Frankham, J. (2003) 'Making sense of the development of inclusive practices'. *European Journal of Special Needs Education* 18(2): 227–242.

Ainscow, M., Booth, T. and Dyson, A. (2004) 'Understanding and developing inclusive practices in schools: a collaborative action research network'. *International Journal of Inclusive Education* 8(2): 125–140.

Ainscow, M., Booth, T., Dyson, A., with Farrell, P., Frankham, J., Gallannaugh, F., Howes, A. and Smith, R. (2006) *Improving Schools, Developing Inclusion.* London: Routledge.

Bartolome, L. I. (1994) 'Beyond the methods fetish: towards a humanising pedagogy'. *Harvard Education Review* 54(2): 173–194.

Blatchford, P., Bassett, P., Brown, P. and Webster, R. (2009) 'The effect of support staff on pupil engagement and individual attention'. *British Educational Research Journal* 35(5): 661–686.

Booth, T. and Ainscow, M. (2002) *The Index for Inclusion,* 2nd edn. Bristol: Centre for Studies on Inclusive Education.

Carrington, S. (1999) 'Inclusion needs a different school culture'. *International Journal of Inclusive Education* 3(3): 257–268.

Copland, M. A. (2003) 'Leadership of inquiry: building and sustaining capacity for school improvement'. *Educational Evaluation and Policy Analysis* 25(4): 375–395.

Corbett, J. and Slee, R. (2000) An international conversation on inclusive education. In F. Armstrong, D. Armstrong and L. Barton (eds) *Inclusive Education: Policy, Contexts and Comparative Perspectives.* London: David Fulton.

Davis, P. and Florian, L., with Ainscow, M., Dyson, A., Farrell, P., Hick. P., Humphrey, N., Jenkins, P., Kaplan, I., Palmer, S., Parkinson, G., Polat, F., Reason, R., Byers, R., Dee, L., Kershner, R. and Rouse, M. (2004) *Teaching Strategies and Approaches for Pupils with Special Educational Needs: A Scoping Study.* London: DfES. Research Report 516.

Dyson, A. (2006) Beyond the school gates: context, disadvantage and 'urban schools'. In M. Ainscow and M. West (eds) *Improving Urban Schools: Leadership and Collaboration.* Maidenhead: Open University Press.

Dyson, A. and Millward A. (2000) *Schools and Special Needs: Issues of Innovation and Inclusion.* London: Paul Chapman.

Dyson, A., Howes, A. and Roberts, B. (2004) What do we really know about inclusive schools? A systematic review of the research evidence. In D. Mitchell (ed.) *Special Educational Needs and Inclusive Education: Major Themes in Education.* London: RoutledgeFalmer.

Elmore, P. L., Peterson, P. L. and McCarthy, S. J. (1996) *Restructuring in the Classroom: Teaching, Learning and School Organisation.* San Francisco: Jossey-Bass.

Fullan, M. (1991) *The New Meaning of Educational Change.* London: Cassell.

Hargreaves, D. H. (1995) 'School culture, school effectiveness and school improvement'. *School Effectiveness and School Improvement* 6(1): 23–46.

Hargreaves, D. H. (2003) *Education Epidemic: Transforming Secondary Schools Through Innovation Networks*. London: Demos.

Harry, B. (2007) The disproportionate placement of ethnic minorities in special education. In L. Florian (ed.) *The Sage Handbook of Special Education*. London: Sage.

Hart, S. (1996) *Beyond Special Needs: Enhancing Children's Learning Through Innovative Thinking*. London: Paul Chapman.

Hart, S. (2003) Learning without limits. In M. Nind, K. Sheehy and K. Simmons (eds) *Inclusive Education: Learners and Learning Contexts*. London: Fulton.

Hart, S., Dixon, A., Drummond, M. J. and McIntyre, D. (2004) *Learning Without Limits*. Maidenhead: Open University Press.

Hiebert, J., Gallimore, R. and Stigler, J. W. (2002) 'A knowledge base for the teaching profession: what would it look like and how can we get one?' *Educational Researcher* 31(5): 3–15.

Howes, A. and Ainscow, M. (2006) Collaboration with a city-wide purpose: making paths for sustainable educational improvement. In M. Ainscow and M. West (eds) *Improving Urban Schools: Leadership and Collaboration*. Maidenhead: Open University Press.

Huberman, M. (1993) The model of the independent artisan in teachers' professional relationships. In J. W. Little and M. W. McLaughlin (eds) *Teachers' Work: Individuals, Colleagues and Contexts*. New York: Teachers College Press.

Kugelmass, J. (2001) 'Collaboration and compromise in creating and sustaining an inclusive school'. *International Journal of Inclusive Education* 5(1): 47–65.

Kugelmass, J. (2004) 'Leadership for inclusion: a comparison of international practices'. *Journal of Research in Special Educational Needs* 4(3): 133–144.

Lewis, A. and Norwich, B. (2005) (eds) *Special Teaching for Special Children: A Pedagogy for Inclusion?* Maidenhead: Open University Press.

Lipman, P. (1997) 'Restructuring in context: a case study of teacher participation and the dynamics of ideology, race and power'. *American Educational Research Journal* 34(1): 3–37.

Messiou, K. (2006) 'Understanding marginalisation in education: the voice of children'. *European Journal of Psychology of Education* 21(3): 305–318.

Miles, S. (2009) Creating conversations: an inclusive approach to the networking of knowledge about education in Southern contexts. PhD thesis. Manchester: University of Manchester. Available online at: http://www.eenet.org.uk/resources/docs/Miles_Creating_ConversationsPHD.pdf (accessed 25 January 2010).

Miles, S. and Kaplan, I. (2005) 'Using images to promote reflection: an action research study in Zambia and Tanzania'. *Journal of Research in Special Educational Needs* 5(2): 77–83.

Robinson, V. M. J. (1998) 'Methodology and the research-practice gap'. *Educational Researcher* 27: 17–26.

Rosenholtz, S. (1989) *Teachers' Workplace: The Social Organisation of Schools*. New York: Longman.

Rustemier, S. and Booth, T. (2005) *Learning About* The index *in Use: A Study of the Use of* The index *for Inclusion in Schools and LEAs in England*. Bristol: Centre for Studies on Inclusive Education (CSIE).

Schein, E. (1985) *Organisational Culture and Leadership*. San Francisco: Jossey-Bass.

Skidmore, D. (2004) *Inclusion: The Dynamic of School Development*. Buckingham: Open University Press.

Skrtic, T. (1991) *Behind Special Education: A Critical Analysis of Professional Culture and School Organization*. Denver: Love.

Slee, R. (1996) 'Inclusive schooling in Australia? Not yet'. *Cambridge Journal of Education* 26(1): 19–32.

Stigler, J. W. and Hiebert, J. (1999) *The Teaching Gap*. New York: The Free Press.

Thomas, G. and Loxley, A. (2001) *Deconstructing Special Education and Constructing Inclusion*. Maidenhead: Open University Press.

Trent, S. C., Artiles, A. J. and Englert, C. S. (1998) 'From deficit thinking to social constructivism: a review of theory, research and practice in special education'. *Review of Research in Education* 23: 277–307.

UNESCO (2010) *EFA Global Monitoring Report: Reaching the Marginalized*. Paris: UNESCO.

Wenger, E. (1998) *Communities of Practice: Learning, Meaning and Identity*. Cambridge: Cambridge University Press.

Part I

Analysing contexts

In order to respond positively to learner diversity, teachers have to understand how children and young people experience what is on offer within the school. This also requires that they identify and address barriers that may be making it difficult for some students to participate and learn.

The chapters in this first part illustrate how evidence of various forms can be used to analyse school and classroom contexts in order to identify such barriers and determine resources that can be used to address these difficulties. These examples focus on a range of contexts and stages of education.

A feature of all the accounts is the way the authors explore innovative ways of understanding the experiences of learners. So, for example, in addition to well-established research methods, such as questionnaires, observation and interviews, the authors explore the use of drawings, photographs, games, learning walks, video recording and mind mapping.

In Chapter 1, Annita Eliadou describes how children's drawings can shed more light on social interaction within schools than would have been possible using more traditional methods of educational research. Building on the experience of conducting a collaborative school-based inquiry in England, she used sociometric techniques in Cyprus to represent children's social interactions diagrammatically and to analyse friendship patterns in relation to their ethnic backgrounds.

Chapter 2 provides a detailed contextual analysis of an extremely diverse inner city primary school responding positively to the effects of poverty, migration and poor health, while engaging with the government's school improvement requirements and its own internal change agenda following the appointment of a new head teacher. The research methods Michele Moore used to carry out her investigations – observations and interviews – are familiar. However, as a researcher in the school who also worked for the local authority, her inquiry required her to address various dilemmas.

Then, in Chapter 3, Debra Martin describes research she carried out to gather the views of teenagers in a pupil referral unit about their experiences in secondary schools. The methods she used to break down possible barriers between young people and adults were particularly interesting in that they allowed her to capture their views on a very sensitive topic.

In Chapter 4 we read Clare Millington's account of her detailed investigation of the efforts of a rural primary school to include one child who uses a communication aid. Finally, Chapter 5 moves to a very different context in considering how Harriet Rowley and Sarah Butson dealt with the challenges of encouraging a pupil-voice approach to research and development in a special school for refugees in India.

Chapter 1

Using children's drawings to explore barriers to inclusion in Cyprus

Annita Eliadou

This chapter illustrates how children's drawings can yield rich data on social interaction within schools. It focuses on a study carried out in a primary school in Cyprus using sociometric techniques to analyse children's drawings. This allowed social interactions amongst children to be represented diagrammatically in order to determine patterns and discrepancies in relation to children's ethnic backgrounds. The chapter demonstrates how drawings can be used to portray aspects of children's everyday school experiences that might have not been readily accessed or explored though the use of more traditional methods of educational research.

In this chapter, I explain how children's drawings can be used to investigate the topic of social interactions within schools catering for highly diverse student populations and the presence of friendship patterns as these develop in relation to children's ethnic backgrounds. While studying for a Master's degree at the University of Manchester, I had the opportunity to participate, along with three other colleagues, in a school-based inquiry project carried out in a school which catered for a multi-ethnic student population (Eliadou *et al*. 2007a). As was discovered while doing research at this school, the school staff collaborated in taking great measures to ascertain that *all* students at the school were included in all aspects of their everyday school experiences. Attention was paid to: ensuring the *presence* of all students at school on a daily basis; giving students opportunities for *participation* both during in-class activities and extracurricular activities; motivating them to *achieve* well academically; and encouraging a climate in which all students were *socially included* at school.

This was a school where students were made aware of each other's national identities, the difference in languages spoken and the different cultures and customs existent in the school. Nonetheless, the school principal showed an interest in investigating in greater depth the topic of *social inclusion*. His concern lay with the fact that students from the same ethnic background seemed to socialize independently of students from other ethnic backgrounds during break time. This piece of school-based inquiry was therefore preoccupied with identifying whether the social inclusion of students was compromised in any way due to the multi-ethnic character of the school, and, in case this was true, in exploring what the reasons giving rise to such findings might be. Hence, this project demanded the identification and use of a research method that would enable the investigation of students' social interaction at school. The method adopted was a drawing technique followed by procedures of sociometric analysis, which allowed the diagrammatical representation of students' social interactions at school. This research method identified that students from specific ethnic backgrounds were socializing in segregated groups. The findings suggested that even a school, which at first glance seemed to be very inclusive, still had a lot to struggle for in order to offer its students a more inclusive educational experience (Eliadou *et al.* 2007b).

Following this project, and for the purpose of my Master's dissertation, my attention turned to the educational experiences offered to students within the educational system of Cyprus (my country of origin), which had only recently attempted to implement principles of inclusive education (Koutrouba *et al.* 2006). Moreover, this educational system had to face the challenge of having to respond to the increased student diversity (ethnic, linguistic, religious) arising from the increased immigration rates recorded in Cyprus over the previous two decades (MOEC 2005; MOEC 2008). I wondered, therefore, whether it would be appropriate to use the same research method, used in a school in England, to investigate social inclusion in a school in Cyprus? If schools in England, dedicated to promoting principles of inclusive education were still struggling to promote inclusion amongst their students, what would I find in Cyprus?

The use of drawings as a research tool

The use of drawings within the research design employed for my Master's dissertation was aimed primarily at presenting a research tool to explore social interactions within a school with a multi-ethnic character, which, in addition, promoted "student voice." It has been evident that in recent years there has been a growing emphasis on involving students in the research process, since children are considered to be both worthy of investigation and as having the right for their "voice" to be heard (Einarsdottir *et al.* 2009). Researchers preoccupied with using research in ways that enhance "student voice" have attempted to identify innovative research methods that provide the researcher with the potential to carry out research *with* children, rather than *on* children (Mitchell 2006; Thomson 2008).

Since researchers within the realm of social sciences have been searching for innovative methods that align with the conceptualization of children as social agents and cultural producers (Mitchell 2006), there has been a renewed interest in research involving children's drawings. In addition, recent research has moved away from the psychological stance of describing children's drawings in terms of developmental sequences, and toward considering children's expressions of meaning and understanding (Einarsdottir *et al.* 2009). Nonetheless, there have been relatively few published studies that have used drawings as an innovative, alternative way to understand children's knowledge and experience; and even fewer where children are invited to be co-interpreters (or narrators) of their own images (Leitch 2008).

When researchers have used drawings within their research, they have been provided with an invaluable tool for the elicitation of children's perspectives on their life experiences, especially when children are encouraged to discuss their drawings (Einarsdottir *et al.* 2009; Leitch 2008; Mitchell 2006; Thomson 2008). Incorporating drawings in research has been useful since drawing is an activity that children engage with in their everyday lives (Einarsdottir *et al.* 2009) and thus they find pleasure in it (Einarsdottir *et al.* 2009; Leitch 2008; Mitchell 2006; Thomson 2008); it does not require the use of complex technology (Mitchell 2006); and is particularly effective to use with children that have difficulties with verbally expressing themselves (Eliadou 2007; Eliadou *et al.* 2007b; Thomson 2008).

This latter characteristic proved to be highly constructive in this study, since it meant that the drawing technique would not offer a "communicative disadvantage" to the participants (Mitchell 2006). Most of the student participants in this study had been recent arrivals to the case study schools and had not yet acquired basic linguistic skills in the Greek language, which is the official language used in the educational context of Cyprus. Thus, using an image-based research technique proved to impose less linguistic demands on the participants and was therefore more enjoyable to participate in. Moreover, relying on the production of visual rather than text data minimized the strain placed on the researcher when trying to interpret and analyze the data collected, since children offered interpretations of their own drawings.

An example of exploring children's social interactions through the use of drawings

While conducting research in Cyprus, one primary school and one secondary school served as case studies and, therefore, as examples of schools that catered for highly diverse student populations. In each of the case study schools the student participants were given a drawing task and were asked to record the names of "close friends" and the names of "other friends," using a pre-planned drawing task arrangement. Different drawing arrangements were presented to primary school students and secondary school students to make the task more age appropriate. At each school each participant had

15 minutes to complete their drawing. The drawing task was presented to 60 students at the secondary school and required that students recorded the names of five "close friends" and the names of five "other friends" (Figure 1.1).

The drawing task presented to students at the primary school was less complicated and required that 40 students drew themselves and their friends and that they recorded the names of the friends presented in the drawing (Figure 1.2).

All drawings were collected at the end of the task and analyzed in an attempt to explore the nature of the social relationships formed at the specific schools in terms of how responsive students were to the increased student diversity. Students were subsequently asked to comment on their drawings and their social interactions at school in a focus group discussion that took place after data from the drawing task was analyzed. I have not retained any of the original drawings that the children produced since one of the conditions of participation at the schools was that all drawings that included personal information would be destroyed for ethical reasons at the end of

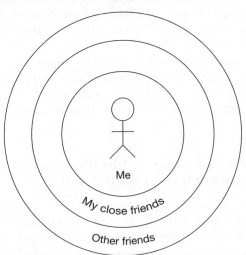

Social relationships in schools
Please mark the names of the friends you have at school.
Give your full name in the inner circle, mark the names of your close friends
in the second circle and in the outer circle the names of other frineds that you have.
Thank you!

Me

My close friends

Other friends

Figure 1.1 This figure represents the drawing task undertaken by students at the secondary school. The students were asked to name themselves and their friends in terms of preference (distinguishing between "close friends" and "other friends"), in this pre-planned drawing task arrangement.

Drawings and Social Relationships

Please draw the friends that you have at school.
Give the full name of your friends and mark your name on the back of the drawing.
Thank you!

Figure 1.2 This figure represents the drawing task undertaken by students at the primary school.

the research project. Only one such drawing was retained for the purpose of presenting the complete research method as it was used in each of the participating schools (Figure 1.3), but during such presentations students' personal information was removed.

Creatively analysing children's drawings to explore barriers to inclusion

Receiving the drawings from students provided me with copious amounts of data to be analysed. Prior to analyzing the data the names of all students depicted in the drawings were coded in order to preserve the anonymity of the student participants. The codes assigned to students indicated the students' gender, age and ethnic background, but provided no additional information that would allow anyone having access to the research to trace any information back to any of the student participants. However, each code was unique to each student so that if information about a specific participant was required by the researcher it would have been possible to trace this information back to the original drawings. An example of a completed drawing, along with the respective covering of names and assignment of coding to replace the names of students in order to maintain the participants' anonymity is presented in Figure 1.3.

Drawings and Social Relationships

Please draw the friends that you have at school.
Give the full name of your friends and mark your name on the back of the drawing.
Thank you!

Figure 1.3 Drawing produced by a primary school boy. The names of his friends have been covered and substituted with the respective codes assigned to each student for the maintenance of students' anonymity.

Since the drawing task employed in this study yielded data that was in a visual format, it was considered appropriate to choose a method of data analysis that would preserve the image-based nature of the collected data. Data was therefore analyzed within a sociometric analysis framework to produce a pictorial representation of students' social relationships in each of the case study schools. Sociometry holds a prominent place in the research literature relevant to children's social development (Bukowski *et al.* 2000). Bukowski *et al.* (2000) claim that sociometric analysis should account for the two fundamental sociometric dimensions of *acceptance* and *rejection*, as indicated by the strong positive or negative links respectively that a student has with members of his/her peer group.

According to this framework, when studying social networks it becomes apparent that there are people who are highly liked by most peers; people who are highly disliked by most peers; and people who are liked by a few and disliked by a few peers (Bukowski *et al.* 2000). Since the arrangements observed within social networks in school contexts are indicative of the *social inclusion* and *exclusion* of students from these networks, an in-depth analysis of the social relationships depicted in the drawing task was under-taken. Bukowski *et al.* (2000) suggest that the two techniques that produce measurements of *acceptance* and *rejection* within social networks are the *nomination technique* and *rating scales*. The *nomination technique* involves students being asked to identify peers to whom they are attached (index of *acceptance*), and peers whom they dislike (index of *rejection*). The *rating scales* involve students' evaluation of each of their peers using a scale which adopts terms representing liking and disliking.

The drawing task employed in this study made use of the *nomination technique* when asking students to nominate their friends and thus indicate the peers with whom they are socially interacting at school. The drawing task constituted measures of *acceptance* but no direct measures of *rejection*. The rationale for avoiding the use of measures of rejection was that in the context of the small classes that served as my sample classes, this might have had the negative effect of enhancing the exclusion of some students – if such a phenomenon was taking place at the school – by directly revealing their *rejection* by other peers. To compensate for not accounting for measures of rejection, the focus group discussions, which involved students in discussions of their drawings and their social relationships, were used to shine more light on the social inclusion and exclusion of students in their respective schools.

Crosnoe (2000) suggests that if researchers can map out the social relationships of students in order to trace direct links between the peers the students nominate as friends, then the researcher can capture the social world of the students. Hence sociograms were constructed in order to represent diagrammatically the social arrangements depicted in the drawings produced by the student participants (Figure 1.4, Figure 1.5, Figure 1.6).

Interpreting social interaction from sociograms

The sociometric analysis and subsequent construction of sociograms essentially allowed the creation of a pictorial representation of the social relationships of students within each of the case study schools (Bukowski *et al.* 2000). The drawings and sociograms provided the tool used to explore social interactions at school, and essentially provided the means to investigate whether students in the schools studied were responsive to increasing student diversity in terms of their preferences for social interaction. The sociograms produced allowed me to identify what the nature of the social interactions was in the specific classes in which I conducted my research. Each sociogram was considered to represent a snapshot in time of the social relationships of students of the sample class. To enhance the credibility of the analysis of the findings from the sociograms, these findings were not analyzed in vacuum but were subsequently analyzed in combination with findings that had emerged through other research methods employed within this research design, such as those of observations and focus group discussions.

More precisely, though, the sociogram of the *primary school* (Figure 1.4) revealed that all students in the class selected other classmates as friends. No student thus appeared to be socially isolated within the class social setting, and all students appeared socially included. Nonetheless, when students were asked to draw "all" of the friends they had at school, no student from the sample class drew as a friend students from any other class besides their own

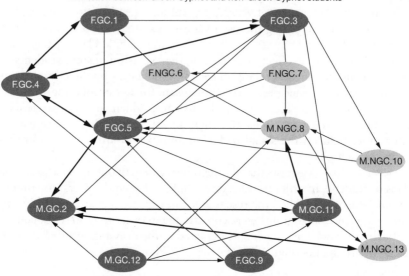

Figure 1.4 This sociogram offers a diagrammatic representation of the social relationships of the children in the primary school studied (*dimotiko*). In each
oval, the code representing each of the 18 students that returned a
drawing appears. Males and females are depicted by the characters "M"
and "F" respectively. Dark gray ovals and the characters "GC" represent Greek-Cypriot students, who are native to the island of Cyprus,
and light gray ovals and the characters "NGC" represent non-Greek-
Cypriot students. Projecting from the ovals are arrows indicating the
preferred friends of the students.

classroom. It therefore appears that the students in the sample class were
somehow restricted to forming friendships only with the other 12 people of
their own class. While the students seem to be socially inclusive in their social
relationships between classmates, the image painted for a broader aspect
of social inclusion at the school was not as positive. This created concerns
regarding the social arrangements at place in the school for the establishment
of social contact between the wider student population.

The most "popular" person in class as it appears was a Greek-Cypriot girl
(code: F.GC.5), who was selected as a friend by 11 out of her 13 classmates,
followed by a Greek-Cypriot boy, who was selected as a friend by six other
classmates. All three non-Greek-Cypriot boys in the class were selected by
at least one Greek-Cypriot classmate as a friend. One of them (M.NGC.8)
was even selected by two Greek-Cypriot classmates as a friend, of whom
one (M.GC.11) appears to be a close friend, as seen by the double arrow

Sociogram of the secondary school studied (gymnasio)

Distinction between Greek-Cypriot and non-Greek-Cypriot students and their close friends

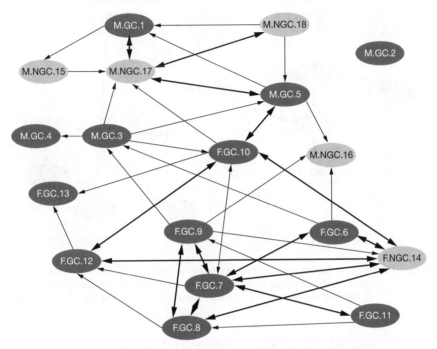

Figure 1.5 This sociogram represents the social relationships formed in the sample
class at the secondary school (*gymnasio*) studied. These relationships
depict the selected "close friends" of the students. See Figure 1.4 for key.

connecting them. But no Greek-Cypriot classmate selected a non-Greek-
Cypriot girls as a friend. Despite the fact that the non-Greek-Cypriot girl
indicated that they have Greek-Cypriot girls as friends, the relationship
does not appear to be mutual, as seen by the absence of double arrows connecting them. The single arrow relationships indicated that one student (a
non-Greek-Cypriot girl) presented another student as a friend, but this relationship was not mutually reciprocated by the selected friend (Greek-Cypriot
girl). Essentially, Greek-Cypriot boys appeared to be more socially inclusive
of non-Greek-Cypriot boys, than Greek-Cypriot girls were of non-Greek-
Cypriot girls.

The sociogram of the *secondary school* (Figure 1.5), depicting the classmates that students consider to be their "close friends," presented a classroom
where Greek-Cypriot and non-Greek-Cypriot classmates selected each
other as friends. Only one non-Greek-Cypriot student (M.NG.18) did not
appear to be selected by any Greek-Cypriot classmate as a friend. The social

Sociogram of the secondary school studied (gymnasio)

Distinction between Greek-Cypriot and non-Greek-Cypriot students and their 'other' friends

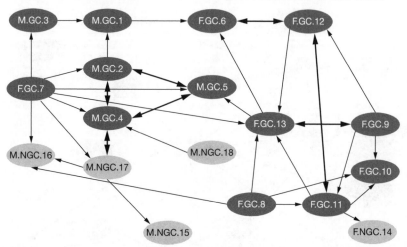

Figure 1.6 This sociogram represents the social relationships formed in the sample class at the secondary school (*gymnasio*) studied. These relationships depict the selected "other friends" of the students. See Figure 1.4 for key.

inclusion of non-Greek-Cypriot classmates by Greek-Cypriots was evident in that the most "popular" girl in class was non-Greek-Cypriot. Despite the fact that she was the only non-Greek-Cypriot girl in her class, she was being selected as a *close friend* by six other Greek-Cypriot girls. Only one person in the class (M.GC.2) was not selected by any classmate as a close friend. At a first glance, this student could have been considered as an isolate, and thus as socially excluded within the social context of his classroom. Nonetheless, when taking a closer look at the sociogram of "other friends" (Figure 1.6) he appeared to be chosen by his classmates as a friend.

The aim of asking students to distinguish between "close friends" and "other friends" was to identify whether Greek-Cypriot students would consider non-Greek-Cypriot students as people they could socialize with, even if not to such an extent as with close friends. Indeed, the third sociogram has shown that Greek-Cypriot students who had not selected any non-Greek-Cypriot classmates as "close friends" (i.e. M.GC.4 and F.GC.11), have subsequently proceeded to indicate that they consider some non-Greek-Cypriot students as "other friends." The fact that most non-Greek-Cypriot students appeared to have Greek-Cypriot friends indicated that the social interactions within this class setting were inclusive and respective of the ethnic, linguistic and religious diversity.

Practical concerns when using drawings as a research method

Despite the positive elements incorporated within research designs using children's and young people's drawings as evidence of "student voice," concerns have been raised about the use of these methods. Leitch (2008) offers an extensive account outlining such concerns; the protection of participants' identities, for instance, is particularly pertinent when collecting visual data. Researchers should reflect carefully upon their ethical purpose, experience, training and capacity for facilitation and support when considering the inclusion of image-making and narrative in their studies (Leitch 2008).

Amongst the ethical responsibilities of the researcher lies the need to obtain informed consent for student participation. Moreover, researchers using drawings have to ensure that a "safe container" is established within the research process. This is achieved through: clarifying the boundaries of who will be involved and how their images will be used within the research project; establishing specific timings within which the research will take place; informing students that there is no right or wrong image; and emphasizing that no higher value will be placed on the esthetic merit of the images when selecting whose "voice" is going to be heard. Finally, it is essential that the researcher responds dynamically to children's drawings by being genuinely interested in the child's images and their ideas about what is going on in the image and what meanings they ascribe to them, rather than trying to identify a "correct answer" to the question posed based on the researchers' own interpretations (Leitch 2008).

Conclusion

This chapter has introduced the use of image-based research techniques, such as children's drawings, which led to the creation of visual images along with sociometric analysis in such a way that it yielded rich data to portray social interactions within schools that cater for highly diverse student populations. This method was developed through participation in a collaborative school-based inquiry and was further explored in the educational setting of Cyprus in a separate research project. This account has demonstrated that drawings can be effectively used to explore sensitive aspects of children's everyday school experiences, such as social interaction and social inclusion at school, which might have otherwise not been accessed or explored through more traditional methods of educational research.

Incorporating drawings within the realm of educational research has proved to be useful for many reasons. Drawing is an activity that children engage with in their everyday lives, and in which they usually find pleasure. It does not require the use of complex technology, and it is particularly effective when used with children who have difficulties expressing themselves verbally. Drawings therefore proved to be a powerful tool for communication between researcher and research participants both in the English and the Cypriot context. Most student participants in both projects were non-native and had not yet fully developed the linguistic skills required to verbally communicate in the official language of instruction used in each of the respective schools. Using an image-based research technique, therefore, proved less linguistically demanding on the participants and was therefore more enjoyable. Nonetheless, it became evident that image-based research should be used with caution and specific measures need to be taken to ensure that such research projects are ethically conducted.

References

Bukowski, W., Sippola, L., Hoza, B. and Newcomb, A. F. (2000) Pages from a sociometric notebook: an analysis of nomination and scale rating measures of acceptance, rejection, and social preference. *New Directions for Child and Adolescent Development*, 88, pp. 11–26.

Crosnoe, R. (2000) Friendships in childhood and adolescence: the life course and new directions. *Social Psychology Quarterly*, 63, 4, pp. 377–391.

Einarsdottir, J., Dockett, S. and Perry, B. (2009) Making meaning: children's perspectives expressed through drawings. *Early Child Development and Care*, 179, 2, pp. 217–232.

Eliadou, A. (2007) Responding to student diversity: two cases in Cyprus. Unpublished Master's dissertation. Manchester: University of Manchester.

Eliadou, A., Lo, W. M., Servio, S. and Simui, F. (2007a) Using children's drawings to investigate racial inclusion in a school in England. *Enabling Education Network Newsletter*, 11, pp. 8–9. Manchester: Enabling Education Network (EENET).

Eliadou, A., Simui, F., Ming, W. L. and Servio, S. (2007b) An evaluation of racial inclusion at FASM school. Unpublished Master's assignment. Manchester: University of Manchester.

Koutrouba, K., Vamvakari, M. and Steliou, M. (2006) Factors correlated with teachers' attitudes towards the inclusion of students with special educational needs in Cyprus. *European Journal of Special Needs Education*, 21, 4, pp. 381–394.

Leitch, R. (2008) Creatively researching children's narratives through images and drawings. In: P. Thomson (ed.) *Doing visual research with children and young people*, pp. 37–58. London: Routledge.

Mitchell, L. M. (2006) Child-centred? Thinking critically about children's drawings as a visual research method. *Visual Anthropology Review*, 22, 1, pp. 60–73.

MOEC, 2005. *Annual Report 2005*. Cyprus Ministry of education and Culture, Nicosia. Accessed on: 27 January, 2007. From: http://www.moec.gov.cy/etisia-ekthesi/pdf/Annual-Report-2005-EN.pdf

MOEC, 2008. *Inclusion in the Cyprus educational system at the beginning of the twenty first century: An overview – National Report of Cyprus*. The Ministry of Education and Culture, Republic of Cyprus, Nicosia. Accesed on: 8 June, 2009. From: http://www.ibe.unesco.org/National_Reports/ICE_2008/cyprus_NR08.pdf

Thomson, P. (2008) Children and young people: voices in visual research. In: P. Thomson (ed.) *Doing visual research with children and young people*, pp. 1–20. London: Routledge.

Chapter 2

Understanding the role of leadership in responding to diversity

Michele Moore

> The complexities of poverty, migration and poor health have a major impact on schools in urban contexts. This chapter tells the story of how an inner-city school, serving an extremely diverse population, engaged with the requirements of the national improvement agenda following a negative inspection report. The school had a tradition of excellent pastoral care, combined with an emphasis on high academic achievement introduced by a newly appointed head teacher. The chapter raises the question of whether sustainable change is possible, and how schools can continue to develop, when their performance comes under continual scrutiny.

Unless we address the issue of school culture in a direct way there is little chance that school improvement will be achieved.

(Hopkins *et al.*, 1994, p. 85)

My interest in school improvement began some years ago when I was teaching in an inner city primary school, judged by Ofsted to be under performing and placed in 'special measures', following an inspection. A school in special measures is subject to the criteria and monitoring arrangements that require Her Majesty's Chief Inspector to 'arrange for the inspection of all schools' (Ofsted, 1999, p. 1). Following the inspection, a report is published and where the school is judged to be failing – or likely to fail – to provide an acceptable standard of education, it is made subject to special measures. This judgement is based on criteria set out in the Framework for the Inspection of Schools (Ofsted, 1993).

This meant that the school became directly accountable to what can be seen as a harsh audit regime. In response to this accountability, intense pressure was put on teachers to improve their teaching, and in so doing, improve academic attainment. As a result, the teachers felt that they were being blamed for the school's failure and that they were not doing a good job. Inevitably, this had a negative effect on staff morale and made it increasingly hard for us to be motivated to work on the improvement agenda. In addition, a rigid timescale was imposed on the school to demonstrate its improvement. This meant, of course, that not only was raising academic standards the priority, but that all efforts were focused on standards. Consequently, other aspects of school life, such as staff development and pastoral care, were largely neglected.

All of this made me even more conscious of how national policy views of improvement have played a significant role in encouraging the audit culture within schools. In particular, I saw how it uses the test and examination success of pupils in order to make judgements about school effectiveness. An improving school, according to these criteria, is one that moves in an upward direction in the league tables on the basis of its test results. Motivating staff to raise the academic standards of those children who are working at significantly lower levels than the majority of the children therefore becomes the main focus for a head teacher.

Although the government claims that there has been an improvement in national test results, there is evidence that many students are marginalized, particularly those from economically deprived areas and from certain minority groups (Ainscow and West, 2006). Some researchers have called this kind of improvement, in which schools have to prove their competence by the power of audit, as 'quick fix' improvement (Stoll and Myers, 1998). They argue that improvement efforts are focused on raising pupils' attainment without developing sustainable systems at the same time to support that improvement. My experience of working in such a school was that although it was indeed possible to improve the test results, sustaining that improvement would prove to be far more problematic.

Urban school improvement

When I moved to a post as a local authority consultant, working to support school improvement, these earlier career experiences informed my interest in finding effective ways of carrying out my new duties. I found that many of the schools I visited faced challenges associated with a highly mobile and economically deprived population. However, through working in different schools I have come to realize that we cannot assume that the challenges facing all schools in the inner city are the same. Rather, the issues faced by individual schools can and do vary according to the school context. I therefore came to the conclusion that if we want real school improvement in our schools, we must move beyond a 'one size fits all' approach to supporting improvement in these schools.

I began to question whether the solution to real and lasting improvement in schools could indeed be found in the relatively simple solution of focusing almost entirely on raising pupils' standards of attainment. Or, are there other significant factors which impact on improvement, for example, leadership, staff collaboration, systems and policies? What are the factors that influence school improvement in schools facing complex contexts within inner cities? To conclude then, my experiences as a practitioner suggested to me that the issue of school improvement is very complex.

Given my experience of working as a class teacher in a failing inner city school, I was interested in exploring issues of school improvement in a different school context. More specifically, my intention was to explore the role of leadership in school improvement by engaging with, and inquiring into, a school with which I was not involved in a professional sense, from my new perspective as a researcher. The primary school I chose for my research, which I shall call Wesley School, had been identified by the local authority and by Ofsted inspectors as an 'improved school'.

Statistical evidence suggested that this school was indeed improving in audit accountability terms. I was, therefore, interested in finding out how the school had achieved its improvement in test scores. How did the staff feel about this process? What kind of leadership was involved?

As a practitioner and researcher I engaged with staff and parents to gain an understanding of their views on the school's improvement. In this way I wanted to see if I could identify a common agreement in the school on what had been achieved and how it had been achieved. I was also very interested in finding out if the improvement agenda had caused any tensions amongst the staff and, if so, how or whether these had been resolved. And, through these investigations, I hoped to draw conclusions that would assist me in carrying out my work as a local authority consultant.

Understanding the school context

Although it is sometimes appropriate to identify common challenges facing schools in urban contexts, it is not fair to assume that all inner city schools face the same challenges. In rather general terms, Ainscow and West (2006) describe such schools as those whose populations are

> drawn from the poorest and least advantaged sections of the community . . . schools where parental income and employment levels are low, where the national populations of ethnic and social minority groups are over-represented, and where there are sometimes significant numbers of bilingual learners.
>
> (p. xiii)

Describing such schools, the Ofsted Report *Strategies to Promote Educational Inclusion: Improving City Schools* (2000) notes:

> They have in common a preponderance of families on low income, in poor housing and with little experience of education beyond compulsory

schooling. Only a small minority of parents work in the professions; many are in low paid manual or service jobs or unemployed. In some cases families are exceptionally troubled. The communities are affected, to different degrees, by bleak surroundings and poor facilities, by poor health, by dislocation and disaffection, and by high levels of alcohol and drug abuse.

(p. 10)

Certainly, in my experience, the majority of children attending inner city schools do live in communities that face many of these issues associated with areas of deprivation. For example, many live in single parent families, often with a large number of siblings, and their parents and grandparents are likely to have been long-term unemployed. The picture, then, for these children is one of poor life experiences, extreme poverty and low expectations.

The population of Wesley Primary School has similar features. The school is situated close to the centre of a large city in the north of England. At the time of my inquiry, it had 176 pupils on its roll, aged 3–11 years, with one class per year group. The percentage of pupils eligible for free school meals was 82.5 percent – over four times the national average. Free school meals is used as an indicator of poverty in a family, so this would suggest that many families whose children attend the school are experiencing extreme poverty.

A major challenge for the staff in this school is the extremely mobile nature of the pupil population – 46.6 percent of the school's population were classified as mobile in 2004/5. This means that over half the children leave the school before they are 11 years old and other children join the school at any time during the school year. For example, of the 30 children in Year 6 taking the statutory tests at 11 years old, only 10 of these children had attended the school for the last four years. All teaching staff, therefore, have the additional pressure of settling, both academically and socially, a significant number of children into their classes mid-year.

Over 90 percent of Wesley's pupils are from minority ethnic groups, the most significant of these groups being Black African pupils, who make up 58 percent of the school population. A significant challenge relating to the ethnicity of the school population is that 79 percent of the minority ethnic pupils speak English as a second language, and a significant proportion are asylum seekers who are experiencing some form of trauma in addition to not speaking English.

Although many inner city schools have large numbers of children for whom English is a second language, 79 percent is an unusually high proportion. In Wesley School these children make up the majority of the school population. It is reported that over 100 languages and dialects are spoken by the children, and so the teachers face considerable communication challenges. A key responsibility for the school leadership is to apportion enough money from the school budget for tuition in their home languages.

At the time of my inquiry, our local authority had one of the worst school attendance records in the country. Attendance at Wesley had also been poor but the figures had begun to show an upward trend and in the year of my research (2004/5) the school met the attendance target set by the local authority.

In 2005, 12.4 percent of pupils in the school were identified as having a special educational need requiring additional resources. In spite of the budget implications for additional staff to support these children, the school is nevertheless responsive to the local authority's request to admit 'hard to place' children; that is, those who may require further additional resources and alternative teaching methods. It is important to recognize that not all schools within the local authority respond positively to requests of this nature. An example of 'hard to place' children at Wesley School were the ten children from traveller families and one child who was being looked after by the local authority. These children require a lot of extra support, both pastoral and academic, in order to raise their attainment from a low baseline level, which is largely a result of their highly mobile and often chaotic lifestyle (Moore, 2006).

What emerges from this contextual analysis is a picture of a school which undoubtedly has many of the negative characteristics of an inner city school, but which also faces the very real additional and complex challenges presented by a highly mobile, extremely economically deprived population, many of whom do not speak fluent English. Extreme poverty, together with these other negative factors, provides a major challenge to staff at Wesley School. And, as we know, the impact of poverty tends to be more severe in inner city environments which, in turn, exacerbates the educational disadvantage experienced by the young people who live there (Young and Melnick, 1988).

In addition to an unstable pupil population, Wesley Primary School had gone through a period of considerable leadership instability until the appointment of the new head teacher, three years prior to the inquiry. During the previous three years, there had been four different head teachers. Such instability in leadership can have a very destabilizing influence on a school and be a major contributing factor to staff insecurity and lack of motivation.

When 'Michael', the current head teacher, took up post, the percentage of children achieving government targets in the statutory tests was extremely low. For example, the average point score of children achieving a Level 2B (the government target for 7 year olds) in mathematics in 2003, was 34.5 percent. There had been a continuous improvement in pupils' attainment during the three years of Michael's headship, so that the same average point score for maths had risen to 60.7 percent.

In addition to these pupil attainment scores, schools are required to publish 'value added' attainment data; that is, data in which pupils' progress is calculated taking into account a range of pupil and school characteristics. This is commonly known as 'contextual' value-added data. Wesley School had shown consistent improvement over three years, in both younger and older pupils, on data calculated in this way, most markedly in science and in particular for lower achieving pupils.

Immersing myself in the school

The main part of my inquiry was carried out intensively during a period of one week. My approach was that of a participant-observer; this meant that I supported both teachers and children in the classrooms, whilst engaging staff in social dialogue at the same time as making informal observations. In other words, I tried, as far as possible, to experience the school life and the school community as an 'insider' (Nias, Southworth and Yeomans, 1989).

Reflecting my professional interests as somebody whose role now was to support schools like Wesley, I focused my research on the following questions:

• What are the factors that influence improvement efforts in schools facing challenging contexts?
• How can staff in such schools engage with these factors?
• What does this suggest about moving schools forward?

During the week I experienced the school in some considerable depth, as I was able to spend time with every class and with each teacher. This gave me an opportunity to appreciate the needs of the pupils, at the same time as observing how members of staff approached the task of trying to respond to these needs. This role required much sensitivity on my part, not least because I was aware that many of the teachers had grown tired of, and defensive about, being observed.

Keeping a record of my experiences was a particular challenge, as I immersed myself in the life of the school, making observations at the same time as interacting with staff and children. I wanted to experience what *normally* goes on in the school. For this reason I did not take notes, nor did I do any formal observations, as my worry was that this could have created feelings of mistrust amongst the staff. I did, however, write a reflective diary at the end of each day. I found, though, that it was important to jot down key phrases during the day, although I avoided doing this in front of staff in the classroom as far as possible.

In addition to observing and talking to staff, I felt that I needed to scrutinize relevant documentation. The school statistical data were of value insofar that they provided evidence of improvements in relation to the national reform agenda. It was important, too, to consider these data when analysing the views of staff on general improvement and in reflecting on the process of change in the school.

Understanding the data, and gaining an understanding of where the school was at and where it had come from, was crucial in order to interpret the views of those within the school community. My study of documentation also included reports, such as the school's Ofsted report.

In engaging with the staff in the school I wanted to challenge my own thinking and experiences of school improvement. In so doing, I kept reminding myself that schools consist of 'a complex web of values and beliefs, norms, social and power relationships and emotions' (Stoll *et al.*, 2001, p. 47).

A dual role

I made an initial visit to the school in my new dual role as researcher and local authority employee. Michael gave me a tour of the school and introduced me to all the staff. I was worried that this might make the teachers unwilling to open up to me. I wrote: 'did they see me as being on the head teacher's side?' (diary entry). Fortunately, as far as I could tell, this did not happen, and after my second visit I noted: 'I feel much more comfortable today. The staff are smiling at me and I am beginning to feel that I am part of the staff.'

I felt it was very important to gain the trust of the staff. At the same time, I was conscious of the fact that becoming too close and too involved could be detrimental to my role as a researcher. Here I was conscious of the advice of Nias, Southworth and Yeomans (1989), who warn that when one becomes an insider one can lose the ability to record and comment with detachment. This became evident to me, for example, when I was observing a lesson and the teacher asked me to evaluate it. Given what I was trying to do, I knew that it was vital that in my role as a researcher I did not appear to be judgemental about an individual teacher's skills. Although it was rather flattering to think that I had built up a trusting relationship with this member of staff, I needed to be detached enough to retain my outsider view, in order to be able to reflect on her practice without having an emotional stake in it. On the other hand, as Nias and her colleagues also note, until the observer does become something of an insider, there is much that they fail to perceive and understand.

Ideally, what I wanted to do was to become involved, whilst at the same time retain the perspective of an outsider. In other words, I wanted to be able to combine an outsider's perspective with an insider's understanding. In practice, my reflections were always based, to some extent at least, on my own interpretations of what I saw and heard. For example:

> I'm not sure that the staff really appreciate what a hands-on head teacher Michael is . . . . Do they know what a plus this is?
>
> (diary entry)

During my time in the school, I thought of its overall atmosphere as combining what I felt to be both a functional and emotional quality. Interestingly, a number of the staff described the school as having what they saw as a 'special quality'. This led me to speculate on where this had come from.

Although, as I have explained, the school has a very mobile population, there are families who have attended the school for generations. Some children have parents, grandparents and in some cases even great grandparents who attended the school. Those members of staff who have worked in the school for many years (one teacher had taught in the school for 30 years, another for 22 years) had taught successive generations of the same families. They explained to me that many ex-pupils come back to work in the school as teaching assistants, lunchtime organizers and kitchen staff because they hold the school in great affection. One of the parents told me: 'This is the best school in the area . . . they [the teachers] are better here than at other schools.'

The word 'special' was used over and over again by staff in their conversations with me. It seemed to me that this demonstrated their feeling of ownership and, indeed, their desire to be protective of the school. Interestingly, even newer members of staff expressed similar emotions. I came to understand more about this through a comment made by a newly qualified teacher who had joined the staff after Michael had become head teacher. She referred to him as the new head teacher, but did not describe herself as being new.

Reflecting on the staff's sense of ownership of their 'special' school, it seemed to me that the head teacher was seen as being different to other members of staff: a person outside the overall feeling of belonging. One colleague commented: 'Even without a head teacher . . . everyone functioned, staff and children.' It was also interesting that many of the teachers agreed that changing the head teacher had not changed the 'special' quality of the school, because they felt that the school 'is bigger than any one person working there'.

Working as a team

When I talked to some of the teaching assistants, I asked them to name some factors which made Wesley such a good school. They all agreed that the most important factor was the sense of teamwork. For example, one replied: 'A good staff who work really well together as a team and really listen to each other.' Interestingly, this was also the view of one of my local authority colleagues, who provided me with an outsider view: 'The staff work well as a team and this is one of the strengths of the school.'

The newly qualified teacher was keen to explain to me how supportive her colleagues have been towards her: 'When you ask another colleague for help, you feel very safe . . . you don't at all feel like a failure.' She felt that there was no feeling of being judged by colleagues. Rather, she and her colleagues felt genuinely safe in asking one another for advice and support, and did not feel that as a consequence this reflected on their own skills, either in a teaching or pastoral sense.

It struck me, too, that there seemed to be little indication of a feeling of the importance of hierarchy amongst the staff; rather, I sensed considerable trust in, and care for, each other as colleagues. Indeed, throughout my observations it was noticeable how staff continually demonstrated ways in which they valued one another. I noted in my diary: 'The staff are very considerate to each other, and no matter which group I am with in the staffroom I never hear anyone gossiping about each other. Teaching and non-teaching staff are impossible to tell apart in the staff room.'

I think it is important to mention here that the lack of importance attached to hierarchy in the school meant that both teaching and non-teaching staff saw each another as colleagues who had expertise to contribute. At one point I noted: 'The office administrator was often to be found in the classrooms and today I discovered she is part of the steel band team' (diary entry).

There is no doubt in my mind that this sense of trust and mutual openness had somehow been developed through talk. At the same time, it was interesting to consider its impact on the core business of teaching and learning. The staffroom was used predominantly as a social gathering place – the conversations there were usually personal, and only rarely professional. In this way, I speculated, the staff had developed close personal relationships which underpinned their professional relationships. However, this meant that they did not use much of their time together to reflect on, or discuss directly, issues related to their teaching. So, although they had developed close personal bonds, they did not have what Rosenholtz (1989) calls a 'consensus about school life'. Nor, as far as I could tell, had they developed a shared language around teaching and learning of the sort referred to in the Introduction of this book.

Michael seemed to be aware of this. He explained to me that he would still like the staff to 'be more reflective, by engaging in more professional dialogues'. He wanted to encourage them to be more articulate about their practice so as to encourage more sharing of expertise. One way he saw this developing was for staff to engage in coaching relationships with each other. I noted an example of what he had in mind in my diary: 'The numeracy lesson was proving very hard for the children to grasp and he [Michael] suggested to the [newly appointed] class teacher a different way of teaching the concept. They were able to have a dialogue about this without the teacher feeling as if her teaching was not adequate.'

Other staff were less responsive to such ideas. For example, a long serving teacher told me that she did not appreciate Michael's presence in her classroom: 'She told me there was a lot of monitoring of lessons at Wesley . . . I asked her if this was coaching and she was quite definite when she said no, it was monitoring' (diary entry).

Leadership for diversity

As I have explained, according to the staff, the appointment of a new head teacher seemed to have had little impact on what they called the 'special quality' of Wesley School. Yet his appointment, without doubt, had had a major impact on the performance of the school. His appointment signalled a change of direction and Michael felt it was important that everyone understood his commitment to take the school forward. Indeed, he made a promise to remain as head teacher for a minimum of five years, thus making it clear that his leadership would provide the school with a much needed period of stability.

In taking over, Michael had two agendas: first, the school had to pass its imminent Ofsted inspection, thus avoiding the school being placed into 'special measures'; second, he had to effect organizational change that would impact positively on teaching and learning, in order to raise and sustain academic standards of achievement.

In order for the school to come through the inspection successfully, Michael felt the school had to 'tick the right boxes'. This meant that he had had to make changes straight away: 'We needed to hit the ground running.' This, in turn, had real implications for his leadership style, as he knew he would have to make significant changes without consulting staff.

Although not entirely comfortable with this style of leadership, Michael felt he had no alternative but to adopt an autocratic style in the early days for the sole purpose of getting the school successfully through the inspection. Morley (2006), writing about his own time as head teacher of a school in special measures, echoes Michael's sentiments when describing his style of leadership:

> the trick was to placate the inspectors . . . . This was not necessarily how I would like to work and was against the principles of my leadership vision for the school, being prescriptive, without collaboration and staff ownership. It was, however, a necessary response to be seen to be competent.'
>
> (p. 29)

Michael understood that the staff were demoralized and insecure, making them defensive about their practice, so he recognized that good communication would be vital. But on the other hand, he had to make decisions and he had to make them quickly. The school had to 'improve their test results to prove their competence' (Morley, 2006).

Prescriptive change, arguably, takes no account of people's feelings and is not owned by the people charged with carrying it out. Commenting on this theme, Day *et al.* (1998) note:

> Change that is not internalised is likely to be distorted and temporary. Hence coercive strategies that are imposed, relying on authority rather than encouraging participation can only result in token change. Real

change involves the modification of perceptions and attitudes; and this is more likely to occur if the practitioners are working on partnership sharing in the strategic direction and decision making process.

(p. 75)

The staff were understandably unhappy with this style of leadership. They were also, I heard, mistrustful of Michael as an outsider. They felt he needed to take time to understand the existing school practices in order to recognize their value. But on the other hand, they admitted that Michael's leadership had brought a drive and an impetus which they felt had been lacking previously.

Michael's immediate priorities were to raise the academic attainment of all children and to raise staff expectations of the children's attainment. Although he recognized the excellent pastoral support staff gave to the children, he felt that their expectations of academic attainment were too low. The children, he thought, had not been given a fair chance; for this to happen they needed to attend a school with high expectations and a good academic record. Michael explained further:

> To be fair to the children we needed to work on attainment as well . . . my vision was to improve all pupils' attainment, whilst supporting their emotional and behavioural needs and developing in them independent learning skills.

The staff were very unhappy, since they felt that this was a direct criticism of their teaching and that they had done something wrong. On the other hand, some approved of some of his methods, especially his commitment to social inclusion. Michael explained that this 'meant putting the time in for individual children and to do that you need a high staff–pupil ratio.' With this in mind, he employed extra staff to support teachers in the classroom. The staff saw this as a strong commitment on his part to supporting children, which they endorsed, and they could see that this had contributed to the children's improved attainment.

Although Michael's chosen style had been autocratic in order to get the school through its inspection, he explained that his preferred style of leadership was to be one of the staff team. For example, he was often to be found in classrooms, both as a class teacher and providing support. I also frequently saw him in classrooms, discussing practice and team teaching. I noted: 'It is not his style to judge teachers (in fact he challenged HMI [Her Majesty's Inspectorate] in the early days when they made a judgement on teaching) . . . he really does understand the challenges teachers face and endeavours to be supportive and practical.'

Michael prefers to model rather than direct methods of teaching. For example, he is very keen for the children to become independent learners as a way of sustaining academic standards. I saw how he models this approach, noting: 'What I liked particularly was the way the children had to take responsibility for their own learning and evaluated the lesson at the end' (diary entry). I found myself contrasting these efforts with the use of approaches to improve test results through the imposition of formulaic teaching strategies which, in my experience, risk creating learners who are dependent on teachers.

Although there was evidence that the children were beginning to take responsibility for their own learning, Michael felt that the staff were still reluctant to assume leadership roles themselves, still seeing this as soley the responsibility of the head teacher and deputy head teacher. In conversation with me, he explained: 'They still don't feel responsible . . . they still need to be more pro-active as regards leadership practices.'

Final thoughts

My engagement with the ongoing story of developments at Wesley Primary School provided me with a remarkable opportunity to reflect on my previous experience of working in a challenging school. It also stimulated me to think more deeply about my role as a consultant to such schools.

All of this reminded me of the social complexities that exist within any school, as those involved each construct their own understandings of what happens. So, for example, in this particular school I noted the tensions that seemed to exist in the minds of some staff as they attempted to make sense of being told they were failing in a way that seemed to dismiss the success they had previously had in responding to a very diverse group of children.

Similarly, their sense of ownership and pride in their school made it difficult for them to accept the requirements of an 'outsider' – the new head – even though they could see the sense in some of his ideas. Meanwhile, he too had to wrestle with the tensions created between his natural instinct to lead through participation and cooperation, and his professional judgement that certain things had to be imposed on the school as a matter of urgency.

The experience also reinforced in my mind that the starting point for thinking about improving any school should be with the practices, experience and creativity that already exist within the school itself. Externally driven improvement does not take the school's existing traditions and cultures into account, and can, therefore, often lead to short-term fixes that are likely to have a temporary impact. In this important sense, I am in agreement with Morley (2006), who argues:

> Sustainable improvement must start from the knowledge and under-standings that already exist within the organisation . . . educational improvement that is to be long-term can only be achieved when it has the commitment of the people charged with making the change happen.
>
> (p. 34)

Research on educational achievement concludes that long-term school improvement needs the commitment of the people charged with making it happen (Stoll *et al.*, 2001). If teachers do not feel a sense of ownership for the changes that are introduced in their school, they will, I suggest, be reliant on the continued presence and direction of the head teacher.

References

Ainscow, M. and West, M. (eds) (2006) *Improving Urban Schools, Leadership and Collaboration*. Maidenhead: Open University Press.

Day, C., Hall, C. and Whitaker, P. (1998) *Developing Leadership Practices in Primary Schools*. London: Chapman Publishing.

Hopkins, D., Ainscow, M. and West, M. (1994) *School Improvement in an Era of Change*. London: Cassell.

Moore, M. (2006) Improving inner city schools. Unpublished Master's dissertation. Manchester: University of Manchester.

Morley, A. (2006) The development of leadership capacity in a school facing challenging circumstances. In M. Ainscow and M. West (eds) (2006) *Improving Urban Schools, Leadership and Collaboration*, pp. 24–34. Maidenhead: Open University Press.

Nias, J., Southworth, G. and Yeomans, R. (1989) *Staff Relationships in the Primary School: A Study of Organisational Cultures*. Cassell: London.

Ofsted (1993) *The Handbook for the Inspection of Schools*. London: The Stationery Office.

Ofsted (1999) *Lessons Learned from Special Measures*. London: The Stationery Office.

Ofsted (2000) *Strategies to Promote Educational Inclusion: Improving City Schools*. London: The Stationery Office.

Rosenholtz, S. (1989) *Teachers' Workplace: The Social Organization of Schools*. New York: Longman.

Stoll, L. and Myers, K. (eds) (1998) *No Quick Fixes: Perspectives on Schools in Difficulty*. London and Washington, DC: Falmer.

Stoll, S., MacBeath, J., Smith, I. and Robertson, P. (2001) The change equation: capacity for improvement. In J. McBeath and P. Mortimore (eds) *Improving School Effectiveness*. Maidenhead: Open University Press.

Young, L. J. and Melnick, S. L. (1988) Forsaken lives, abandoned dreams: what will compel us to act? *Harvard Educational Review* 58(3): 380–394.

Chapter 3

Reflecting on the experience of mainstream education

Exploring pupils' views in a pupil referral unit

Debra Martin

Woodfield Pupil Referral Unit was established to provide an education service for pupils with medical or emotional needs. It caters for secondary age pupils who have been referred by Child and Adolescent Mental Health Services, and sometimes by schools. This chapter provides an account of the way learners at the unit conducted an inquiry with one of their teachers. Students at Woodfield have been marginalised from the education system: many have spent a great deal of time out of school, yet this is not because of disciplinary reasons. The main focus of the inquiry was to examine the students' perceptions of their mainstream schools through focus groups, questionnaires and peer interviewing. Two clear themes emerged from the research: the lack of supportive relationships with staff and the students' feelings of lack of safety in large mainstream schools.

I got more and more scared and afraid of going, and worried about what would happen if I did go. When I did go in, you just get people asking 'Where have you been?' 'Why have you been off?' They don't really care, they're just being nosy.

Views such as this are rather typical of those I sometimes hear from the students I teach at Woodfield Pupil Referral Unit (PRU). I decided I wanted to know more about their experiences in the schools they had previously attended in order to see if this would help in deciding what needs to happen to improve the situation.

Undertaking research in the place where I teach provided me with some significant advantages over researchers who go into schools as outsiders: I already had positive relationships with the students and staff; I had knowledge of how the school operates; I had support from the staff; and as I was in the school every day, it was relatively straightforward to proceed with the inquiry. As I discussed my proposals with my colleagues, I found that they were also keen to find out more about the students and how they feel about being at Woodfield.

Although there has been a growing recognition in English schools of the importance of encouraging learners to express their views about their education and for these views to be taken seriously, there are some learners whose voices are less likely to be heard. For example, Arnat and Reay (2007: 313) talk about 'students and adults at the margins of public schools' and the need to elicit their 'silenced voices'. These include: children with disabilities; children not living at home; children who have been excluded from school; and children who simply do not attend school (Curtis *et al.*, 2004).

The students at Woodfield remain formally enrolled in schools across the local authority, even though most of them have missed a significant amount of school. This is due to sporadic attendance or complete non-attendance – in some cases for over a year. My inquiry therefore set out to explore the educational experiences of Woodfield students prior to being referred to this specialist facility.

Context of the inquiry

Most pupil referral units are primarily for pupils who have been, or are, at risk of being excluded from mainstream schools due to their behaviour. Woodfield is therefore unusual since it caters for learners who have not attended school because of either medical or emotional reasons.

The unit serves a local authority on the edge of a large northern city that has a number of areas of social deprivation. This is where the majority of students live. Although the local authority has an ethnically diverse population, this is not reflected in the intake of pupils at Woodfield, who are almost exclusively from white, working class backgrounds. At the time of the inquiry, boys outnumbered girls almost two to one, although historically the intake has been more evenly balanced.

Woodfield operates on two sites: a small classroom based at the local hospital which provides education for pupils from reception to Year 11 who have short-term medical conditions; and the main site, where the inquiry took place, which is a converted office block. At the time of the inquiry there were 36 pupils on roll at the main site. The building does not look like a school and this helps some of the more nervous pupils feel at ease. It has a quiet, calm atmosphere and although the lack of space has been recognised as a problem at times, it can also contribute to the pupils feeling safe. Unfortunately, due to its small size, Woodfield cannot possibly offer the variety of subjects and extracurricular activities offered by a mainstream school.

The main site provides an education for:

- Students who have emotional and social difficulties relating to a negative school experience, previous long term illness and other traumatic life experiences. They have often had significant absence from school.
- Students waiting for places in mainstream or special schools. These are often young people who have moved from another authority; a number are children in local authority care.
- Students who are too ill to attend school. These students attend Woodfield on a part-time basis in order to complete work set by their mainstream school.
- Students for whom the local authority has no other provision. Sometimes this includes those who are regarded as being 'at risk of exclusion' from their mainstream school for disciplinary reasons. These students are effectively excluded from their school, and remain on the roll of their original school even though it is clear that there is no intention for them to return.

The majority of referrals to Woodfield come from Child and Adolescent Mental Health Services, while others come from medical and psychiatric consultants, schools, learning mentors, education welfare officers and the coordinator of the pupil referral unit service. The length of time that students are on roll at Woodfield can vary from a few days in the hospital classroom, to two or three years for a pupil who can not be reintegrated back into school. The average length of time spent at Woodfield for the young people involved in this study was about nine months. Although officially there is only one reason given for their referral, in reality students tend to arrive with an assortment of mental health issues, family problems and difficulties faced in their mainstream schools.

Rationale for the inquiry

Learners who are not able to attend school miss crucial aspects of academic work, but they also miss out on social and emotional aspects of their development. As a result, as time goes by they often become increasingly isolated and may lose touch with school friends. Woodfield offers such learners a second chance at education and the opportunity to be with, and learn alongside, other young people.

This inquiry was an attempt to find out more about how the learners at Woodfield perceive their mainstream schools and to explore what implications this might have for their reintegration back into mainstream education. Woodfield offers a rare opportunity to conduct research into the reasons why some young people have effectively excluded themselves from school. These young people have an important and usually unheard perspective on mainstream schools: 'It is crucial for students to know and feel that they, the experiences which have shaped them, and their modes of showing are recognised, respected and valued' (Arnat and Reay, 2007: 318, citing Bernstein, 2000: 174). This inquiry was a first step in giving these young people a voice. The primary research question was: *How do pupils feel about their mainstream schools?*

Woodfield caters for some of the most marginalised young people in our society. If we are to effectively include them and, indeed, improve our schools for all learners, we need to know about their experiences and perceptions of mainstream schools.

Learners as co-researchers

A secondary purpose of my inquiry was to try and evaluate *peer interviewing* as a research method. This approach had not been used at Woodfield before. Enabling the students to conduct interviews, and act as co-researchers by encouraging the involvement of other young people therefore represented a big step.

I wanted to involve as many students as possible in the study and I felt that using a wide variety of methods would facilitate this. I therefore chose to conduct a focus group, distribute questionnaires and support the carrying out of peer interviews. I was also conscious that the use of different methods for collecting data would strengthen the credibility of my research.

A *focus group* was held with one of the Year 11 groups with six young people aged 15–16 years and their teaching assistant. We discussed the factors that they felt might be significant in students choosing not to go to school.

Four themes came out of this:

1 **Difficult relationships with teachers.** For example, stressful experiences in some subjects, such as physical education, were reported.
2 **Bullying.** They argued that the fear that this created was the worst thing. They also thought that schools could be scary because they are too crowded and busy.
3 **Health issues.** Students reported that it would be embarrassing to admit to mental health problems as they would have to answer lots of questions. Similarly, if they had been off school for a long time, they were likely to have to answer questions.
4 **Family reasons.** For example, some students were responsible for the care of family members.

The majority of students (20 out of 36) completed a *questionnaire* asking them to consider how they felt about Woodfield and about their mainstream schools. In response to questions about their mainstream schools, the majority reported that they did not miss anything, but six said that they missed friends and two missed the opportunity to study a wider variety of subjects. Three-quarters of the students stated that they would not like to return to their original schools, but two clearly wished to return, and one felt that he could return since his problems had now been identified.

A quarter of the students chose not to answer the question about why they stopped going to school. Of those who did: five reported bullying and four mentioned depression or anxiety. Other reasons cited were: illness, poor relationships with teachers, teachers who were unsympathetic, hating school, family problems and difficulties in coping with the pressure of academic work. Only one student had been formally excluded for disciplinary reasons. Almost half said that they had not kept in touch with anyone from their former school.

Key words and phrases used to describe the advantages of being at Woodfield included: 'friendlier', 'calmer', 'more support', and 'quieter'. Four students mentioned the lack of bullying, the safe and secure environment, its small size and fewer pupils. One mentioned making new friends and another making a fresh start.

Students were asked to complete the sentence, 'If there was one thing I could have changed about my school it would have been . . .' The answer given by the majority of the pupils was 'the teachers'. The disadvantages of studying at Woodfield were identified as: the restricted number of GCSEs available, its small size, the small number of young people with whom they can socialise, and the lack of freedom.

In addition, I used *peer interviewing*. Here, my main idea was to demonstrate to the students that the inquiry was about them – that it would help them to get their voice heard and to take some ownership of the project. I spoke to a number of Year 11 pupils about acting as interviewers and four expressed an interest in taking part. Subsequently, two of the initial four decided not to take part, so I proceeded with two peer interviewers. I had a meeting with my co-researchers to agree on the questions to ask, to discuss any issues that might arise during the interviews, and to ensure that they understood the ethical issues involved, such as confidentiality, and the procedures around disclosure if one of their peers were to disclose anything sensitive.

Altogether, ten students were interviewed by the two male co-researchers, who tape recorded the interviews and later transcribed them. The selection of the ten students was determined by their availability at the time of the interviews. Both peer interviewers were a little nervous about interviewing their peers, as this was their first experience. Interestingly, though, they added insightful questions as a follow up to the agreed questions. They were also sensitive to the feelings of their peers and made it clear that interviewees did not have to answer any questions which caused them to feel uncomfortable.

The peer interviewers began by asking how students felt about attending Woodfield. Responses were mostly positive, for example: its small size, good relationships with staff, and students get into less trouble with teachers and other pupils than they did in their mainstream school. Negative aspects included: missing friends from school and the restricted curriculum. The findings therefore reinforced evidence I had collected from the questionnaire and focus group. Only one student said he did not feel that he belonged, and he is the only student who had been excluded for disciplinary reasons. He explained that the other students 'don't do the stuff I do, or like the same stuff that I do'.

When asked to describe their original school, the students used words such as 'busy', 'unfriendly', 'noisy', 'scary', 'squashed' and 'unsupportive'. One student described how he had felt lonely, and another that he did not feel safe. Two students used more positive language about their original schools and said that they missed them. A wide variety of factors were cited as preventing school attendance, including family issues, crowds in school, bullying, depression and being excluded. In response to the question, 'Who could you speak to at your old school if you were having problems?', the answer from all ten students was 'no one', and 'I couldn't speak to anyone there'. When asked to describe how they would feel if they were told they would be returning to their mainstream school, the majority (eight) used words and phrases such as 'worried', 'anxious', 'angry', 'scared', 'devastated' and 'I'd refuse, I wouldn't do it'. By contrast, the one who had been excluded for disciplinary reasons said that he'd be 'buzzing! [excited]'.

Although this experience of peer interviewing was a positive one, not least because of the way the two students played a key role in deciding on the interview questions and collecting the data, they were not involved in any data analysis. I was concerned that rather than being involved as co-researchers, their involvement could have been interpreted as tokenistic and that the inquiry had been teacher-led. After all, I had to write a formal research report which would be examined as part of my Master's degree, and I wanted to do well. Kellett (2005: 3) warns that, 'Participatory research of this kind is still adult designed, adult led, and conceived from an adult perspective.'

Making sense of the inquiry

Young people are usually only referred to Woodfield after several years of experiencing difficulties in their mainstream school, often resulting in them refusing to attend at all. Schools are not always supportive of the students' return as they are frequently seen as problems because of their poor attendance. In the age of performance league tables, schools may not be rewarded for trying to engage with such vulnerable students. At the same time, as I have shown, the students themselves are often not enthusiastic about returning, since they feel that the schools have let them down by ignoring their mental health problems, not dealing with bullying, not giving them adequate support, or overlooking their conflict with particular members of staff. These students have effectively excluded themselves from the mainstream, but they have chosen to re-engage with education at Woodfield.

The themes which emerged from my inquiry tell us a great deal about the broad context in which many children in English schools learn, and fail to learn. In particular they tell us about the importance of developing and sustaining good relationships with students, ensuring they feel safe, and returning them to mainstream schools as quickly as possible.

In relation to this agenda, the main conclusions I have drawn from this study are:

1 Lack of support for vulnerable students in mainstream schools emerged as a key theme throughout the inquiry. Students reported that there was no one they felt they could talk to at school. Small educational settings, such as Woodfield, offer the individual attention so badly needed by students who have emotional difficulties. Cornwall and Walter (2006) argue that some children will always need additional care and support, and a more therapeutic approach to education. For these children the quality of the relationships with the teachers and other staff will have an enormous effect on their ability to access the curriculum. The positive relationships with staff at Woodfield and its small size were mentioned throughout the inquiry.

Students reported that they felt safe at Woodfield, whereas they had not felt safe at their mainstream schools, usually because of bullying. Students spoke of their disappointment when they did seek help in the face of bullying, because nothing happened. Students felt that the anti-bullying policies in schools were not fully implemented with teachers turning a blind eye to what was going on. According to the students, it is 'the bullied' who have to leave school, not 'the bullies'.

However, as Woodfield works with staff in mainstream education to reintegrate some students, students should be entitled to have access to a named teacher, or other member of staff, that they feel they can trust – 'key workers' have previously been identified as a success factor in reintegration (DfES, 2004). Meeting a teacher from the mainstream school for the first time in the safety of Woodfield might be a safe way forwards for anxious students.

2 Many students felt that their education was restricted by being at Woodfield and that they would like to have returned to school if it had been possible. Two spoke about what I describe as the 'snowball effect'. They felt that they could have returned to school if they had had help earlier. However, it became harder and harder to go back, as Stroobant and Jones (2006: 222) confirm, 'School refusers are less inclined to return to school the longer they have been absent; they discover other (rewarding) ways of "being" that do not include being a school attender'. These findings have implications for the reintegration process which needs to be a much swifter process if it is to be more successful. Although schools

are often reluctant to accept students back in the final two years of compulsory schooling – the exam years – they have a responsibility to do so. This is the last chance for such vulnerable students to gain qualifications. Also, from a legal point of view, the majority of students are dual registered on the school rolls of both the mainstream school and Woodfield.

Personal reflections

I learned a lot from carrying out this study, not least about the willingness of my colleagues to provide support for such activities. Specifically, they provided me with lots of practical help in planning the peer interviews, designing and distributing the questionnaires, and preparing the final presentation I was required to give at the university. The teaching assistants attached to each student group were also involved in helping with the questionnaires and the focus group.

However, there were some professional and ethical tensions involved in working as a teacher and conducting research in the same school. Despite their support, at times I felt isolated from my teaching colleagues and guilty about completing research in school time. There was no formal allocation of time for the study, and it was difficult to balance the demands of a full-time teaching job with conducting an inquiry. I was also very conscious of how busy my colleagues are and I sometimes found it difficult to ask for help.

I was very conscious, too, that I did not have the opportunity to observe Woodfield as an outsider. I was already aware of the backgrounds of the students taking part in the inquiry and the reasons for their referrals. I was concerned that knowing the students so well may mean that I could not be objective. Yet, I felt that my lack of objectivity as an insider researcher was also a great strength.

Ofsted has recognised the importance of the positive relationships the students have with the staff at Woodfield. I was concerned that this may make the students hesitant about criticising Woodfield and be more critical of their mainstream schools. However, these relationships have also given the students confidence to be open about their feelings and experiences. I was surprised at how enthusiastic they were about their involvement in the inquiry, and how open and honest they were in their responses. The majority were keen to express their opinions about Woodfield and their previous schools, and several mentioned that no one had ever really asked them what they felt before. At the same time, staff interest in the findings presented me with a confidentiality dilemma, since I was unable to share what particular individuals had said.

Some staff have shown an interest in using and evaluating the peer interviewing technique. Indeed, we have had subsequent discussions about ways of using peer interviewing in future projects, such as involving older students in interviewing younger students about their concerns regarding reintegration. Next time, however, it will not be so teacher-led.

More than anything, this inquiry has provided opportunities for students to reflect on their own and others' experience of mainstream schools. For some, this led to a noticeable change of perspective, from 'I couldn't cope in school', to 'How could school have been different?' In this way, the often hidden voices of these young people have pointed to possibilities for educational improvement that could be of benefit to many others.

References

Arnat, M. and Reay, D. (2007) 'A sociology of pedagogic voice: power, inequality and pupil consultation'. *Discourse: Studies In The Cultural Politics Of Education* 28(3): 311–325.

Cornwall, J. and Walter, C. (2006) *Therapeutic Education: Working Alongside Troubled And Troublesome Children*. London: Routledge.

Curtis, K., Roberts, H., Copperman, J., Downie, A. and Liabo, K. (2004) 'How come I don't get asked no questions? Researching "hard to reach" children and teenagers'. *Child And Family Social Work* 9: 167–175.

Department of Education and Skills (DfES) (2004) *The Reintegration Of Children Absent, Excluded Or Missing From School*. Research Report RR598. London: DfES.

Kellett, M. (2005) *How To Develop Children As Researchers*. London: Sage.

Stroobant, E. and Jones, A. (2006) 'School refuser child identities'. *Discourse: Studies In The Cultural Politics Of Education* 27(2): 209–223.

Chapter 4

Understanding the challenges facing a child with communication difficulties in a primary school

Clare Millington

Finding ways of including children with communication difficulties is a challenge facing more and more schools. This chapter
illustrates and explains the value of analysing the experiences
of an 11-year-old student with physical disabilities who uses a
voice output communication aid in the context of a rural primary school. At the time of the inquiry the student in question was
about to transfer from her primary school to the local comprehensive school.

More specifically, the chapter describes the observation of teaching and communication strategies used by teachers and teaching
assistants in a wide range of formal and informal contexts. The
analysis of the inquiry data threw light on the importance of
involving parents in strategies to help children use low and high
tech communication aids; and the need for staff to recognise
opportunities for non-verbal children to use aided communication. It also revealed that the communication aid was in danger
of simply supporting the curriculum, rather than enabling wider
social exchanges.

Voice output communication aids (VOCAs) have made much greater inclusion possible for children with communication difficulties – VOCAs are the
hardware for communication. However, the hardware itself is a small part of
the solution as children have to learn to use the aids in a variety of situations
in the school setting, and, more importantly, school staff need to be flexible
enough to adapt their own teaching methods and communication styles, so
that the aids can be used to maximum effect in schools.

VOCAs are an example of recent technology developed for use in alternative and augmentative communication (AAC). Signing and symbol boards are
less high-tech examples. Children who use AAC are a diverse, and relatively
rare group of learners, characterised by being largely non-verbal and needing
aids to help them communicate. They may also have learning difficulties, or

physical impairments – where, for instance, their communication difficulties arise from cerebral palsy – or they may have both. The more complex their needs, the wider the range of solutions needed so that they can overcome barriers to communication, and so access the curriculum. However, learning to use AAC can be compared to learning a foreign language that is not used by anyone else in the community – including the therapists and teachers whose role it is to support the inclusion of children with communication difficulties.

My daughter is an AAC user and I have had concerns about the quality of the inclusive provision in our local primary school. My interest in this inquiry was initially prompted by a comment made by a speech therapist visiting my daughter's school in 2006: 'The modern classroom is not set up to encourage verbal communication.' It later transpired that he was referring to the fact that equipment such as scissors and pencils were placed on the children's tables and therefore did not need to be asked for. However, his comment alerted me to the need to investigate whether there was indeed some truth in this statement, and so, my focus in this inquiry was on the question, *How can mainstream environments enable the inclusion of children with communication difficulties in a meaningful way?*

I set out to conduct an inquiry into how an 11-year-old student (who I will call Lucy), was being supported to learn to communicate in a mainstream classroom, and what strategies were in place to support her inclusion. Lucy has physical impairments and is an AAC user. Her parents were anxious about her imminent transfer from her local rural primary school to a large rural comprehensive, and they were enthusiastic about, and supportive of, my inquiry.

My study aimed to collect evidence of good practice that had been accumulated throughout the child's time at primary school with a view to transfering this practice to the secondary school, as appropriate. Lucy's parents were concerned that the many long hours spent using trial and error to find successful approaches to communication would have to be reinvented by the secondary school. Or, it would be up to them, as the constant adults in her life, to transfer the knowledge, as no member of the support staff was being transferred with Lucy. The parents were already anticipating the exhaustion, following the transition, in providing the necessary support and advice to the school. They recounted the efforts they had made to ensure that school staff were trained in the use of signing and low-tech boards with symbols for pointing, and then the hard work involved in obtaining funding for a VOCA and arranging for the subsequent training in its use. Most of this had been put in place because of the continuous pressure they had exerted on the school and local authority.

It is worth adding here that Dr Stephen Hawking has done a great deal to enlighten the public about alternative methods of communicating. In their own way, Lucy and her parents have helped to raise awareness in their own local community.

Using a wide range of methods

Given the complexity of my research agenda, I felt it wise to use a mosaic approach to the collection of data (Clark, 2004). This involved using a wide range of methods, including: observation; photography as a method of visually recording information; photo-based discussions; a learning walk; an interview; and a questionnaire. In this way I was able 'to bring together a complex range of visual and verbal material' (Clark, 2004: 160).

This wide range of techniques gave me confidence that I was getting as broad and accurate a view as possible of the approach to inclusion practised at the school, and of Lucy's views of her school experience. Although Lucy had a good understanding of language, she faced considerable barriers to using rich language, and so it was essential to collect as much data as possible from a wide range of different viewpoints.

Detailed *observation* was essential for getting to grips with the sheer range and complexity of some of the technical assistance provided to Lucy (see Table 4.1 for a summary). This also affirmed for me the parents' concern that the secondary school needed to capture the expertise that had been accumulated through enormous amounts of time and effort. A record of observations could be one such way of capturing this expertise. I chose to be a non-participant observer within the classroom, as I needed all my concentration to record the minutiae of what was happening. Being at the edge of the class, also served to promote my acceptance as a non-threatening figure, and to show the children that it was not just the child with impairments who was under the microscope.

In addition to observing the teaching strategies and techniques used by teachers and one particular teaching assistant (TA) to support Lucy's communication, I used a digital camera to capture key moments. My aim was to capture moments when communication was particularly successful. I hoped that secondary school staff would be able to recognise the techniques in context. Seeing through the lens enabled me to focus on details and allowed us to reflect later on moments that otherwise would have passed in seconds. In this inquiry, therefore, 'I saw my role as co-interpreter rather than sole interpreter' (Clark, 2004: 160).

Much of the information that would have been transmitted by speech was transmitted by signing, pointing and other personalised schemes that were determined by Lucy's physical needs. In this way a photograph could be considered as a form of 'pupil voice' – showing Lucy's optimal ways of communicating, and her desired positioning in relationship to her communication partners. Photography has had a lasting impact on the understanding of Lucy's experience, and was an excellent medium for the immediate and accurate recall of aspects of the school environment. It also enabled the transfer of knowledge of successful teaching strategies to the secondary school, where Lucy is now thriving.

Table 4.1 Observation of strategies for inclusion of an AAC user

Strategy	Example of context in which it was used	Comments
The TA scribes while Lucy uses several modes of communication (sign, choice boards, VOCA) to construct prose.	When Lucy is engaged in creative thought. The flow of creative thought would be interrupted and slowed down if she had to record words by herself, e.g. when writing a poem.	In order to ensure that Lucy's input is not influenced by the TA: • Lucy needs to be assertive • the TA needs to be patient • the teacher needs to trust the process.
The TA translates Lucy's personal signs, and voices them to the class.	When an answer of several words is required quickly. When the VOCA or other physical aids cannot be used, e.g. lunch hall and playground.	It is best if Lucy's signs are seen by all, otherwise there is a danger that her peers only hear the TA's voice. Light reflecting from the VOCA screen prohibits its use outside. The VOCA volume is not loud enough for the lunch hall.
Questions asked requiring the following answers: • yes/no. • true/false • yes/no/maybe • other.	Choice making. Comprehension checks.	The whole class used signs for yes/no/maybe – thumbs up, thumbs down or thumbs sideways.
Random selection of pupils by teacher when asking open questions. E.g. by using a pot of sticks with each child's name written on them.	Open questions requiring a verbal answer.	The 'waiting time' for an answer of more than two words is very long. The strategy of randomly selecting pupils (with sticks) helps to avoid teachers' tendencies to always ask those pupils who answer quickly – rather than asking pupils who may struggle with more challenging questions (including Lucy).

(continued on next page)

Table 4.1 (continued)

Strategy	Example of context in which it was used	Comments
Use of sign to communicate numbers.	Any question requiring a numeric answer, e.g. mental arithmetic, numbered choices.	An immediate way for Lucy to show off her academic ability.
Instruction board.	In test situations (where drawing or rough work is needed), Lucy uses the visual aid (instruction board) to give instructions to the TA to work through the stages of solving a problem, e.g. draw a number line, count on 3, etc.	This approach to tests was developed with the SATs tests on numeracy in mind, but this is now used more generally.
Use of pre-programmed topic words on the VOCA.	For practising the use of new vocabulary and checking the understanding of definitions, e.g. the appropriate use of 'proverb' and 'parable' in religious education.	This requires the TA to work together closely with the class teacher to provide key words before the topic is introduced – i.e. takes time and requires careful planning.
TA spontaneously providing a limited range of word/symbol choices on a small white board.	Deciding which symbol (+, –, x) to use to solve a maths problem.	This helps Lucy choose – but limits her choice.
Pre-made communication boards.	A grid containing likely adjectives for a literacy topic. Times tables boards.	This helps, but limits Lucy's potential for learning.
Symbol use across the class.	Any time a phrase can be replaced by a symbol, e.g. self-assessment using 'smiley faces' or arrows.	Everyone is using the same mode of communication. Peers get some insight into Lucy's use of symbols.
Lucy types answers into the VOCA to use as a verbal answer.	Times when an independent answer is vital. When no easier option is available. For unusual words known to Lucy but to no one else present.	Prior notice of the teacher's question would be helpful. Patience is needed by all in waiting for Lucy's answer. This needs lots of practise, as it is a skill in its own right, independent of classroom activities.

Table 4.1 (continued)

Strategy	Example of context in which it was used	Comments
Input words by typing on the computer.	Practising written literacy skills. TA may type some words from scribed copy to enable work to be finished on time.	TA input necessary to avoid continual failure to complete work. Even if it is only possible to complete a section of the work, Lucy has a sense of closure with the piece of work. This also needs practising as a skill in its own right.
Presentations to the class using PowerPoint.	Presentation was prepared at home to show successes outside school, e.g. weekend at an activity centre. Lucy gave a presentation about herself to promote understanding in others.	Photography important for providing detailed information.
Presentations in assembly and in church.	VOCA can be attached to an amplification system when Lucy is doing readings, or is in the role of a narrator.	Good for introducing a wider audience to a VOCA. Many parents commented on Lucy's inclusion in the harvest service.
Inner voice.	For prayers and song.	Encouragement to focus on meaning and hear the words in her head. Lucy was not keen to sign in assembly.
Play strips (strips of card with images of celebrities/ cartoon characters, etc.).	Chatting about current topics of interest with her peers. Role play.	Dr Who and Harry Potter characters had been popular in Year 5 but Lucy's peers felt they had outgrown this type of play. There is a constant need for updating this kind of material – which can be very time consuming.
Time alone with non-signing adults.	Visiting specialists who do not sign. Replacement teachers or TAs.	This forces use of the VOCA. One-to-one nature of the interaction means that the unknown adults have to be patient. Lucy has control of the conversation with the new adult.

Themes arising from the observation of inclusion strategies

Responding to questions

Many of the strategies had been designed to help Lucy cope with the speed of response needed in a mainstream classroom. This is a problem shared by others with additional needs in the mainstream classroom, whether it is a verbal or written output. It takes an immense amount of time and effort to construct a phrase using AAC, even for someone without additional physical difficulties. Often an answer would be constructed, but it would be too late for the answer to be delivered as the class had already moved on.

The strategy of giving a narrow range of choices (yes/no, true/false, multi-choice) helped Lucy to contribute and show her knowledge to the class, but restricted her opportunities to practise techniques for building new phrases. This strategy could therefore be detrimental to Lucy's academic inclusion. The teachers need to be aware of the need to strike a balance between Lucy's specific need to learn to communicate in more complex phrases, with the need for the class to work at a faster pace for the other children. By continually bypassing the difficulty of providing longer answers, Lucy was not given enough opportunities to learn a skill that would be necessary for other areas of inclusion, such as extended writing and conversation – and, more importantly, for her inclusion in secondary school where the pace would be considerably quicker. Interestingly, Lucy has made remarkable progress in the use of her VOCA since her transition to secondary school.

One of the most successful strategies involved randomly selecting students to answer open questions so that all students, whatever the length of time it took them to reply, had the challenge of answering such questions using rich language. This benefited the whole class, since it stopped the same students from answering again and again, and gave those who were slower to respond a chance to contribute at length without feeling under pressure.

Signing

I observed a tendency for the TA to translate Lucy's signs. This was also accompanied by: an over-direction of activities by the TA; a restriction of conversation to 'adult friendly' topics; and a reduction of conversational opportunities between Lucy and her peers. Lucy's most common communication efforts (verbal output by VOCA) involved signing to 'her' TA. This had, I felt, led to a very close bond between Lucy and the TA, almost to the exclusion of anyone else in the class. This seemed to me to be dangerously isolating for Lucy, given that the TA was not being transferred to the secondary school. Relying on one individual to translate Lucy's signs created an immense barrier to social inclusion.

Signing is immediate, portable and wonderful for those close to the AAC user, and for those who are prepared to invest the time in learning a full signing system. However, an over-reliance on signing as a sole method of communication in a predominantly non-signing world might be considered short-sighted when other AAC methods (e.g. VOCAs or other symbol systems) are available. The speech output of a VOCA can be understood by all and promotes much greater independence. Yet it requires more thought and preparation by the whole teaching staff and considerable effort by the non-verbal students themselves.

Promoting independence

Carrying out tasks for a child in order to promote inclusion can directly conflict with the need for the child to become more independent. Yet, it is more time consuming to teach a child to carry out the tasks for herself – and schools are busy and time-pressured places. Striking the balance between these opposing needs is a difficult job for the teaching assistant and this issue was not often overtly addressed in this inquiry. Individual education plans are often concerned with the 'here and now' of how to tackle academic objectives, rather than thinking ahead to the longer term priorities for a student – such as the transition to secondary school.

In school it may be seen as important for students to produce an answer to a teacher's question within a strict time framework in order to keep up with the class. It is therefore easier to use a TA trained in interpreting signs, rather than to wait for students using communication aids to produce their own responses. In the long term, however, what happens if and when this specialist support is not available? The observation revealed that key personnel have been entrusted with the responsibility of facilitating communication. The school had made a conscious choice to use a TA, rather than to find alternative, more long-term solutions, such as everyone at the school being taught the signing alphabet – a task that takes about 30 minutes. Waiting patiently for answers that take time to construct on a VOCA inevitably poses challenges in busy mainstream schools – yet these challenges have been overcome in Lucy's secondary school.

Disability awareness

The use of symbols by the whole class, and the use of common signs such as thumbs up and down, was very effective at promoting inclusion. Play strips with pictures of favourite television characters acted as a low-tech resource that stimulated discussion and role play for *all* children in the playground, and allowed Lucy to lead in making choices when playing games. In this way, some of the challenges to Lucy's social inclusion in school were tackled.

Social inclusion in the community was also helped by encouraging Lucy to use her VOCA in public performances such as the harvest festival. The parents of Lucy's peers may not have encountered Lucy personally before this event, and were not likely to know anything about AAC. Yet Lucy's parents commented on how delighted they were by the number of people in the community who took time to speak to Lucy after her performance in the festival.

If techniques used for the inclusion of a child with disabilities can be used throughout a whole school (and the wider community), then the understanding of the barriers faced by a student like Lucy can be eased. Their acceptance as 'just another child' can be encouraged. The fear of difference often arises through a lack of understanding of that difference. Most people may be totally unaware of the abilities of a child who uses a wheelchair and does not speak naturally – parents may even discourage their children from playing with them. It is a common assumption that children who cannot speak naturally are also deaf, particularly if they sign, so they are often ignored, or sometimes shouted at rather than spoken to.

Learning walk

Important information was generated through the use of the learning walk techniques. This involved me moving around the school with Lucy to assess how the different environments helped or hindered her communication and participation. While Lucy was happy to use a score sheet and to tell me what modes of communication she used en route, it was too difficult for her to communicate her justification for her scores in words when on the move. This is a good example of one of the major barriers she faces in communication. I therefore photographed each area we visited which was to be scored, so that she could reflect on the area later in a more optimum environment for communication.

I developed the following way of scoring the different aspects of the school context:

The environment makes it:

0 = impossible to communicate
1 = hard to communicate
2 = neither hard nor easy to communicate
3 = possible to communicate well
4 = ideal for communication.

Lucy's preferred environment was her own desk area, where she has a swivel chair, access to her VOCA and room to turn easily to sign to her TA. Here she could communicate with the class and her TA with minimum barriers (score: 4). The ICT corner is where Lucy had access to maximum assistive technology, but was not able to turn easily to sign to her TA (score: 3).

Outdoors – where it was impossible to use the VOCA due to light reflecting from the screen, and activities were more physical allowing ease of use of gesture, some signs and the playstrips (score: 2). From my own observation of children in the playground, activities such as dashing around (even in a walking frame) were quite enjoyable with little formal communication. The hall and library – the VOCA was hard to hear and when the space was used for assemblies it became too crowded to be able to use signing easily with the TA (score: 1).

The learning walk had proved to be an effective means of learning more about Lucy's experiences in the classroom and around the school. In particular, her reflections revealed the complex interplay of the nature of the environment, the demands of the activities to be carried out in those environments and her personal preferences. For instance, I had expected the hall to be quite good for VOCA use, since it has good acoustics, but the activities in the hall (such as school assembly) required children to frequently change the volume of their speech, making the VOCA impossible to use. Also, the TA did not sit next to her in assembly and sign translation was impractical.

A wider sample

In order to draw on a wider set of experiences, I carried out a questionnaire survey of some 50 parents, teachers and other professionals who have knowledge and experience of non-verbal children and who were attending a meeting on a given day. On the questionnaire, I listed a range of classroom practices that I assumed to be common knowledge for supporting inclusion at primary level. But my assumption was incorrect.

Participants were asked to affirm whether the techniques I had listed had been successfully used with non-verbal children. The response from parents was one of indignation and worry, since they could only tick a small number of boxes. In turn, this led to some unforeseen friction between the parents and the professionals. The parents had hoped that the teachers would be fully conversant with all possible approaches. In some cases parents had never heard of the inclusive practices mentioned on the questionnaire, indicating that their children do not discuss what happens at school with their parents. These responses also indicated that the parents had not asked the teachers about classroom practice. I was under the misconception that most parents of children with communication difficulties would want to know about how their child was included, but this was clearly not the case, and I found that I had opened an ethical 'can of worms'.

Although the interviews with teachers had provided rich information on current techniques used with non-verbal children, there was a view from some teachers that the therapists and teaching assistants had the main responsibility for inclusion. Also, there were differences of approach between visiting therapists and teachers that suggested to me that there was very little shared language of practice or knowledge of each other's domain.

Making sense of the evidence

This inquiry examined Lucy's access to the academic curriculum in some detail. The detailed observation and the learning walk were the most successful methods used. The least successful research techniques included interviewing teachers and collecting questionnaire data from parents.

As my inquiry proceeded, I became increasingly aware of how important it was for Lucy to have 'down time'. Students with one-to-one learning support are constantly under the microscope and often being urged to communicate. Thinking (with Lucy) on the learning walk about her activities in the playground revealed to me her relief at having a break from the tiring business of relating to others.

The questionnaire touched upon the concepts of 'circles of friends' and 'peer group training' (Newton *et al.*, 1996) so that I could get a feel for whole school efforts to promote social inclusion. I concluded that Lucy was frequently isolated from her peers and that the VOCA was in danger of becoming a curriculum support machine, rather than an aid to wider communication, as social exchanges were mainly made through translation of signs by the TA. The inquiry had certainly not answered my worries about whether a mainstream school was a good place to learn to communicate if a student has a substantial communication impairment. Rather, it had raised a whole range of new, previously unconsidered, issues.

I felt an enduring sense of unease with the narrow focus of many professionals on Lucy's learning techniques to access the curriculum – rather than on the efforts that could be made by school staff and wider society to find ways to accommodate her. What about the responsibility of the school community to remove barriers for Lucy? How were they helping or hindering her communication by their own actions? Why is it so difficult for people to understand how a VOCA works?

It seems that the final question is far from being answered. Since the technology is relatively new, users are comparatively rare and they often face a variety of other barriers to using their VOCA machines, such as physical difficulties (Soto *et al.*, 2001). To widen my view of the inclusion of VOCA users, I instigated a further inquiry which focused less on the 'hardware' associated with inclusive practice and more on the nature of pre-existing opportunities for VOCA use in a school (Millington, 2008). This current research involves trying to recognise when the peer group is most receptive to helping AAC users maintain conversation in a social context and is taking place in a different rural primary school. Early results show that semi-structured opportunities, such as changing for physical education and morning registration, are far more productive in enabling 'chat' than the less structured times, such as break time, when peers may be involved in faster moving exchanges.

Final reflections

Reflections on my research were greatly aided by keeping a diary throughout the whole process: from my initial thoughts on the topic of the inquiry, to the harrowing process of searching for the right words to explain my findings. My diary captured key aspects of the experience, and enabled me to relive feelings, such as the 'highs' of success, and to wonder at how assistive technology has allowed us to break down some barriers to inclusion. However, it also recorded the frustration and fury at people with set agendas who refused to make small changes to accommodate Lucy.

Coming from a background in applied sciences, I had started my inquiry with a hypothesis, and tried to take an objective stance. However, through detailed reflection on my diary data, I came to realise that staff attitudes, and flexibility and co-operation across the whole school, were as important to Lucy's inclusion as the hardware used in augmentative and alternative methods of communication. These factors were hard to quantify. Assessing their role in the inclusion of a child with complex needs involved acknowledging my feelings, judgements and prior knowledge as a parent of two disabled children. It was necessary for me to admit these feelings in my diary, and consider them as yet another line of investigation in the complex network of factors that help move inclusive education forwards.

References

Clark, A. (2004) 'The mosaic approach and research with young children'. In V. Lewis, M. Kellett, C. Robinson, S. Fraser and S. Ding, *The Reality of Research with Children and Young People*. London: Sage, pp. 142–162.

Millington, C. (2008) 'What factors affect the quality and range of opportunity for voice output communication aid (VOCA) users in the mainstream primary classroom?' Unpublished assignment. Manchester: University of Manchester.

Newton, C., Taylor, G. and Wilson, D. (1996). 'Circles of friends: an inclusive approach to meeting emotional and behavioural difficulties'. *Educational Psychology in Practice*, 11: 41–48.

Soto, G., Müller, E., Hunt, P. and Goetz, L. (2001) 'Critical issues in the inclusion of students who use augmentative and alternative communication: an educational team perspective'. *Augmentative and Alternative Communication*, 17(2): 62–72.

Chapter 5

Promoting student voice in an isolated community in India

Harriet Rowley and Sarah Butson

This chapter provides an illustrative account of how an inquiry-based approach was used to promote student voice in a marginalised community in Northern India. The project was carried out over a two week period in a school for children with refugee status. The aim of the inquiry was to promote discussion of inclusion and exclusion by empowering the students to talk about the barriers they experienced in everyday life and in their learning. The students were able to express themselves through visual representation (photographs), and used the images as a stimulus to explain 'their world'. In this way, they were both the subjects of the research and participants in the inquiry-based approach. Their teachers also participated in the process, and were able to use the evidence collected to bring about change within the school.

One of us (Harriet) had been working as a volunteer for the Enabling Education Network (EENET), which is based at the University of Manchester. This work involved corresponding with practitioners in some of the economically poorest countries in the world in response to their requests for basic information on inclusive education. EENET's main role is to disseminate much-needed documents to encourage policy makers, teachers and children themselves so that they can develop more inclusive and equitable practises in education (Miles and Ahuja, 2007).

Given the challenges of working cross-culturally, EENET has been developing image-based approaches to research and development to support facilitators and practitioners working in remote areas of the world. One of these approaches is known as 'photovoice', or 'participatory photography' (Wang *et al.*, 1996). It is an innovative and remarkably successful approach to working with marginalized groups, as it enables them to communicate their experience through images, and photographs in particular.

Previously we had worked collaboratively on a school-based inquiry project as part of the Master's programme, which investigated the low educational achievement among primary-school-age boys who were eligible for free school meals. Harriet was subsequently commissioned by a special school for children with severe learning disabilities in the north of England to explore the use of participatory photography in promoting student voice. Keen to work together again, and to further explore the use of inquiry-based approaches to research, we approached EENET with our ideas.

Inquiry-based research in a challenging context

EENET made contact with a social development advisor to a refugee community in a rural area in northern India where a special school for children with a vast array of disabilities had recently been established. The advisor was particularly excited about the idea of introducing photovoice principles to support the ongoing research and development work at the school. As a result, the advisor began to prepare for our arrival by developing clear terms of reference for their inquiry, and welcomed our expertise with great enthusiasm.

Figure 5.1 Front gates to the school.

The context of the school presented itself as challenging and exciting: nestled in the foothills of the Himalayan Mountains, it caters for 50 students, aged from 5–17 years, with a variety of disabilities. The majority of the students are boarders, have little to no contact with their families, and originate from a range of neighbouring countries (including Tibet, India, Nepal and Bhutan). The student population is therefore marginalized in a number of ways; not only are they disconnected from their friends and families in their home towns, but they are housed and educated separately from other children living in the area. The children are also a disparate group; some have severe physical and intellectual disabilities, while others have behavioral difficulties.

School staff were also enthusiastic about the prospect; photovoice offered an opportunity to address some of the existing barriers in the school by promoting student voice while introducing a new skill to practitioners, which has the capacity to expand and influence current pedagogy. The school had hosted a variety of practitioners and development workers in the past, and was able to provide accommodation and food. Although the majority of staff and students could understand some English, the school provided two teachers to act as translators throughout the project. We spent several months preparing for the task, with EENET's support and liaising with the advisor in India. The advisor's relationship with EENET was a source of support as we prepared for our two-week stay with the school.

Preparing our photovoice project

The school was interested in understanding the experience of their students and hoped to gain insight into the barriers and facilitators that they faced to learning. It was our role to act as a critical friend, fostering an environment where teachers and students could investigate their own context, typical of inquiry-based approaches to research. Our aim was to use photovoice to create this dialogue in a manner that, ideally, the school could continue to use after we had left.

Crucially, the children would be telling the story from their own perspectives by using photos as a stimulus to explore their thoughts and feelings about their surroundings. Therefore, the inquiry involved photography exercises; sometimes individually, and sometimes in groups, taking pictures of places representing a particular theme. Topics traditionally used in participatory photography include: 'good' and 'not so good,' 'welcoming' and 'unwelcoming,' or 'inclusive' and 'exclusive' places (Kaplan, 2008).

In previous studies, students then engaged in activities that encouraged 'photo-elicitation,' whereby the photos acted as a stimulus for 'reflection, commentary and interpretation' (Kaplan et al., 2007). In other words, the photos are used to explore children's thoughts and feelings, thus enabling them to describe their experiences, giving the listener a unique insight into 'their world.' These conversations are often shared between students and practitioners, but also with the wider school community in an exhibition which extends the reach of the student voice. This means that all stakeholders become involved in a critical reflection about how practises can be changed to ensure that the environment is more inclusive of all learners.

As we both had a background as educators, we knew it was important to include icebreakers and games to allow us to get more comfortable with each other and provide a break from some of the more demanding research activities. We developed a timetable that featured games, ranging from simple activities to learn each other's names, to more complex games designed to enable the children to explore their identity.

We realized we needed to break down the photovoice project into more manageable chunks: introducing how to use a camera; providing examples of photovoice projects conducted in other contexts; brainstorming ideas of 'good' and 'not so good' places around the school; how to take photos using different perspectives; facilitating the taking of photographs; and finally activities that encouraged students to talk about their thoughts and feelings using their images as a stimulus.

It was also important to close the project with an exhibition where the students would present and share their work with the rest of the school community, as this had been a successful strategy in EENET's previous work. Our hope was that this would enable the student's achievements to be celebrated and recognized, while ensuring that practitioners and the school's management team heard the important messages of what the children thought about their school and home environment.

Figure 5.2 Students viewing and discussing photos from projects in other countries.

Adjusting to the context

We arrived in the midst of the hot, sticky and rainy monsoon season and were greeted by the advisor, the school principal and a sea of smiling children. The school and the students themselves were immediately welcoming, presenting a special and humble atmosphere. One of the first hurdles we had to overcome was deciding which children to work with as they were all keen to be part of the project. The teachers in the school were also under the impression that we would be able to work continuously with an entire class (around 30 children), however, we did not have the resources or the capacity to meet this expectation. Therefore, we decided to initially work with the chosen class and ensure everyone had a chance to take part in some of the photovoice work.

Later, we divided the group and chose to work with only ten children. These students were chosen by the practitioners as those who would most benefit from the photovoice project. As the school hoped to continue to conduct similar inquiries of their own in the future, they would target other groups at a later date. Fortunately, by the end of our time at the school, the students had become comfortable enough that many would use the cameras at break time and in the evenings, though not officially part of the project.

After meeting the students and playing some games to get to know them, it became clear we would have to adjust our timetable in order to better meet their needs. Some of the students displayed greater strengths than expected, such as two boys with muscular dystrophy and a girl who had had a stroke. With the right support, these students were able to share some very interesting insights into their experiences and were determined to use this

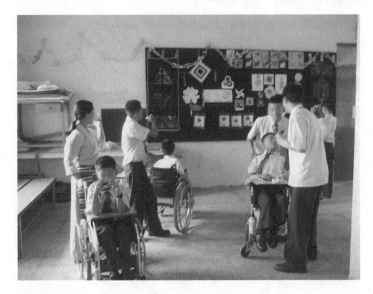

Figure 5.3 Students learning to use cameras.

Figure 5.4 Using mind maps to brainstorm themes.

opportunity to have their voices heard. Others had limited means of communication and understanding, but could still benefit from trying to express themselves using an entirely new and creative forum. One feature which was obvious from the beginning was the closeness of the school community; the teachers and carers knew the children's strengths and weaknesses very well, and the children themselves were also encouraged to help and look after each other. Much of the time, it was a case of trial and error to see what worked.

Once they had familiarized themselves with how to use a camera and the teachers were comfortable with the methodology, we led discussions about places within the school environment the children thought were 'good' and 'not so good.' They were then split into pairs and took it in turns to take photos of the places in the school community that applied to each category. Where necessary, we encouraged students to work in pairs and to support one another. They were also encouraged to think creatively about how they could take a photo to communicate their message as effectively as possible. Once the photos had been uploaded onto the computer in separate files, the students selected to be printed the ones they felt were the most meaningful.

The selected photos were used in a variety of photo-elicitation exercises designed to help the students use the photos to talk about their thoughts, feelings and experiences of education. The photos and descriptions were then presented in a variety of ways, such as posters and mind maps. By the end of the project we had a phenomenal amount of creative work to be displayed in the exhibition and a number of students eager to express their perspectives.

Figure 5.5 Students explaining what their photos mean to them.

Emerging themes

The students took a variety of photos that identified positive and negative feelings associated with the following themes and aspects of their lives: well-being, access and hostel life.

Well-being

Many of the students took photos of the physiotherapy room, the kitchen and the prayer hall, because these were the places where they said they felt most happy. The physiotherapy room was recognized as a haven for some of the students because they had a close relationship with the physiotherapist. Photos were also taken of the kitchen and dining hall because they enjoyed the food and sharing meal times with one another. One student in particular was proud of the role he played assisting the kitchen staff and serving the food. Another highly photographed area was their classrooms. During photo-elicitation exercises many talked positively about their teachers and were proud to be a part of their class.

Access

The children who used wheelchairs photographed the door leading into the physiotherapy room. We later discovered that because the door opened outwards it was difficult for them to gain access independently. This issue was easily rectified during our stay by changing the hinges to ensure that the door could be pushed to open inward. This represented an issue which could be quickly addressed but that had served as a formidable restriction for many of the students. Similarly, many of the paths around the school also caused problems and restricted some children's access to particular areas. Some were rough and uneven, whereas others were slippery when wet causing great difficulty in the monsoon season. Accessing sufficient funds to rectify these larger issues was beyond the scope of our inquiry, but staff at the school were committed to improving the physical environment.

Hostel life

Although the school staff had tried their best to make the accommodation inviting and homely, in reality the dormitories were fairly cramped, had at least ten beds in each and a set of small cupboards. There was limited space for personal belongings. The girls' and boys' dormitories were separate and each one had two house parents, usually a couple with small children of their own who would sleep behind a curtain at one end of the room so that they could provide care throughout the night. There was a variety of practises amongst the house parents; most had little training but despite this many were dedicated.

Some children said that they had few friends in their dormitory, while others identified particular problems with the sleeping arrangements. Narayan, for example, who has particular communication difficulties, took a photo of a bed in his dormitory. To an outsider a picture of a bed has obvious meaning as a place of rest and relaxation. During the photo-elicitation, however, Narayan expressed that the photo was in fact, of the bed next to him. The child who slept in this bed often had unsettling behavior and needed specialist care, consequently keeping Narayan awake. As a result of the participatory photography process, Narayan was moved to a quieter spot. He had been visibly tired, which was affecting his school work and overall well-being.

Figure 5.6 The physiotherapy room – a place the students liked and where they felt comfortable.

Sharing the findings

As the research project drew to a close, we started to think more about how to share the findings with the rest of the school community. Before arriving at the school we had a vague plan of holding some sort of exhibition but were not sure how this would work in practise. We were also apprehensive about how some of the findings would be received and what would be the most appropriate way to both celebrate, what in the children's eyes, the school was doing well, while also identifying what they were not doing so well. Most importantly, we wanted to ensure that the suggestions for improvement were realistic in terms of what the school could afford and were capable of changing. We also wanted to recognize the many outstanding practises in a community which faced considerable marginalization. It was important to involve the students as much as possible and encourage them to present, since this was their exhibition.

After some discussions with the advisor and the teachers, we decided to organize an exhibition where the children who had taken part in the main research project would be the presenters: sharing with the audience their understanding of photovoice and presenting the findings related to well-being, access and hostel life, as well as anecdotal personal accounts of their school experiences.

The actual exhibition surpassed all expectations and proved to be a very powerful device in communicating emotive messages to those who attended. We encouraged the school to invite neighbouring mainstream schools as this was a good opportunity for staff and students to mix with other school

Figure 5.7 The final exhibition – an opportunity to socialize with students from surrounding schools for the first time.

Figure 5.8 The final exhibition: local schools, community members and government representatives.

communities. It would give them the opportunity to share and celebrate their expertise using the new and creative method of photovoice. The school invited the minister of education and other notable community members.

Numerous rehearsals were held with the students, many of whom were not used to such responsibility or speaking on stage in front of an audience. Despite their nerves and difficulties with communication, they showed tremendous courage and determination. Although many of them did not have the means to communicate how they felt about the experience directly, it became apparent that they recognized this was a unique opportunity for them to convey their thoughts and feelings. For some, this was an opportunity they had always longed for but never had. For others, the ability to convey their thoughts was something they had lost as a consequence of their situation.

Such a public sharing meant that the students had to come to terms with their deteriorating health, and their new home which was in many ways disconnected from their previous experiences. The combination of the children's histories, the unique context and the messages they were communicating through photovoice was tremendously powerful. It is difficult to express in words how we felt watching the children on stage and reflecting on our role in their accomplishments. Some of the students' achievements had been anticipated – communicating their experience through visual means – but there were other outcomes which were more subtle and in some ways more significant.

Figure 5.9 Students making a presentation at the exhibition.

An email from the advisor, sent a few days after we left the school, high-lighted the benefits of the project:

> This research project has enabled the children to show what I was sure was inside, but what was sometimes difficult to convince others about – and it's actually been a very moving experience. I've seen reticent children come forward with real strength and confidence. I've seen children given more than a token "voice" for the first time – and others re-discover voices who had maybe lost the sense that anyone was listening. I've seen adults surprised and indeed amazed by children whom they have known for years, and by what they are able to show and to do. I've seen those same adults realising that inside their children are thoughts and ideas which are far deeper, more sensitive and creative than they ever faintly considered. And I've seen all the children . . . grow immensely and almost visibly shine.

Final reflections on a rewarding and challenging experience

Our aim was to act as facilitators, encouraging both practitioners and children to use photovoice as a means to reflect upon their practises and context. This approach seeks to empower insiders, who know their con-text best, by providing them with the tools to make the familiar, unfamiliar (Delamont, 1992). However, outsiders can play a helpful role in assisting insider practitioners to overcome barriers within a particular context – but this needs to be done subtly and sensitively.

Despite good intentions, we found it difficult to foster a situation where we were truly acting as facilitators, rather than leading the research. The practitioners were extremely humble and in many ways unaware of their excellence. Global power imbalances and the recent history of the refugee community were difficult to truly understand within a short space of time. We encouraged the teachers to reflect on their own situation using examples from our own contexts, in the UK and in Canada. We also tried to build their confidence by discussing the failings in our own education systems and by highlighting good practise in their school.

Our dual experience as practitioners and researchers certainly helped us to overcome these hurdles and as time went by we developed a relationship built on trust, and the teachers began to feel confident in their new roles – as researchers. Ideally, we would have continued to support an ongoing inquiry process by visiting the school periodically. However, we were only able to create a brief interruption within the school community. We know that the advisor will do her best to keep the initial spark alive, continue to develop the necessary tools for reflection upon practises and context, and so better cater for all learners in this special school.

References

Delamont, S. (1992) *Fieldwork in Educational Settings: Methods, Pitfalls and Perspectives*. London: Falmer.

Kaplan, I. (2008) 'Ethics and visual research: being "seen" being "heard" engaging with students on the margins of education through participatory photography'. In P. Thomson (ed.) *Doing Visual Research with Children and Young People*. London: Routledge.

Kaplan, I., Lewis, I. and Mumba, P. (2007) 'Picturing global educational inclusion? Looking and thinking across students' photographs from the UK, Zambia and Indonesia'. *Journal of Research in Special Educational Needs*, 7(1): 23–35.

Miles, S. and Ahuja, A. (2007) 'Learning from difference: sharing international experiences of developments in inclusive education'. In L. Florian (ed.) *Sage Handbook of Special Education*. London: Sage, pp. 131–145.

Wang, C., Burris, M. and Xiang, Y. (1996) 'Chinese village women as visual anthropologists: a participatory approach to reaching policy makers'. *Social Science and Medicine*, 42(10): 1391–1400.

Part 2

Making interruptions

In the Introduction, we argued that progress in addressing diversity often demands the development of new thinking and practices within a school. The chapters in this second part illustrate how engaging with evidence can, under certain conditions, create 'interruptions' that challenge existing assumptions and highlight possibilities for challenging and changing policies and practices which may previously have been overlooked. They also illustrate the valuable roles that 'outsiders' (e.g. students studying in universities, advisory teachers; educational psychologists) can play in providing assistance when carrying out such investigations and in offering different perspectives as evidence is analysed.

In Chapter 6, Emma Lindley and her colleagues present an account of an inquiry into the involvement of very young children (3–6 years) in a school council in an urban primary school. It explains a process of action research used to develop approaches that explore how the children can be enabled to have their say. The chapter illustrates ways of capturing the voice of the youngest pupils. With the help of older pupils, they were able to overcome the structural barriers which had prevented the youngest children from participating in the school council prior to the inquiry. The account indicates how the findings of the inquiry challenged taken-for-granted assumptions amongst staff within the school.

Then, in Chapter 7, Pamela Aspin, a behaviour advisory support teacher, presents an account of an inquiry focused on a child-centred intervention to promote pro-social behaviour with young children. The combined efforts of the author, a young and enthusiastic class teacher and a group of five children, known as the 'A' team, were recorded using carefully structured observation techniques, diaries, interviews and a questionnaire. The account is a further striking illustration of how evidence collected through such a study can reveal new possibilities for strengthening practice within a school.

Processes by which evidence can create interruptions are also vividly illustrated by Hannah Scott in Chapter 8. She describes the development of a collaborative approach that enabled young adults with learning difficulties in a further education college to express their views about their own learning.

We read how these contributions challenged the perceptions and assumptions of staff, such that they began to see the students in new ways.

Finally in this part, in Chapter 9 Emma Lindley provides an account of how her penetrating research into the attitudes of a group of teenagers towards mental illness generated some very challenging data. Such material has enormous potential to provoke discussion within a school about policy and practice. However, these discussions would need careful facilitation, since, as we explained in the Introduction, those involved may not be willing to consider ideas that challenge their well-established ways of thinking and working.

Chapter 6

Too young to have a voice?

Exploring how to include young children in a school council

Emma Lindley, Rosanne Brinkhuis and Linda Verhaar

School councils in primary schools are regarded as an effective means of engaging pupils in matters which affect their life in school. However, the structure and configuration of school councils often mean that children can only express their views within a relatively restricted and limiting frame. Furthermore, very young children (3–6 years) are often completely excluded from school councils, on the basis that they are considered to be simply too young to have a view. This chapter describes a project in a primary school that set out to investigate and address this issue, using a range of techniques to enable younger children to express their views on their experiences of school. The authors explain how these approaches enabled the very young to demonstrate their views, thus interrupting the prior assumption that the youngest children were too young to participate.

We worked together to help a primary school explore whether it was possible for the youngest children in the school to contribute meaningfully to the school council. The inquiry took place during the autumn term of 2006, and we tried out research methods designed to be used with young children, and developed our own approach to the challenge.

In order to keep pace with the pupil voice agenda, the head teacher of the school, which we call 'Small Tree', had put in place a school council. However, the minimum age for membership of the council was 7 years, and so children in the Nursery, Reception and Year 1 (aged 4–6 years) were not included. The reason the youngest children were not included was that there was a strong assumption that they would simply not be able to participate in the school council processes, as they had been set up. The common assumption that very young children cannot participate in democratic processes was clearly at play in this context. Yet, as this inquiry shows, the answer to the problem lay in the way the school council was organised. In this way, the inquiry interrupted school practice and caused staff to think differently.

This interruption was made possible by the critical role played by the older pupils in the inquiry.

In what follows we report on how we set about implementing an inquiry-based approach to finding practical solutions, which would help the school to be more inclusive of its youngest members. We begin by briefly introducing the school, and go on to give an account of the process of inquiry we undertook, describing in particular two strategies for listening to the very young which we trialled within the school and a proposed method for including the younger children in school council processes.

Context: the school and the school council

The primary school in which the research took place is a mixed non-denominational school with 436 pupils on roll. It may be of interest to the reader to know that 48 per cent of the pupils at Small Tree come from homes where English is not the first language. Free school meals are received by 15 per cent of the pupils, although the head teacher told us that many more families were eligible to claim them but chose not to do so. The school is located in a relatively affluent city suburb with a strong community identity and is well-served by amenities and services. The population of the suburb is over 87 per cent white, so the ethnic mix at the school is not representative of the demographic dynamics of the surrounding area.

When we began our project, the school council had been in place for almost one academic year; so it was still relatively new, but had been functioning long enough to have established itself. There were 20 elected members on the council, composed of a boy and a girl from each of the two classes per year group, from Year 2 to Year 6. The purpose of the council was to give pupils a voice, enabling them to contribute to the development of the school and to be empowered to make decisions about things which would affect them and their peers. The aim was that the council would act as a vehicle through which children's views could be incorporated into longer term development and planning for the school. The council had a small budget which it could spend and decisions about how this money would be used took place within council meetings.

Locating and focusing our inquiry

We used two main strategies for establishing starting points from which to launch our investigations: talking to staff and pupils to find out more about their understandings of the question of young pupils' voice; and looking at relevant literature.

We spent some time in discussions with the head teacher, as well as the class teachers responsible for the early years' classes. In addition to having conversations with the adults who were around very young children, we also spent some time with the children themselves. We carried out observations in each of the early years' classes, and this helped us to get a general sense of the ways in which the children interacted with one another, and with the adults around them.

From the interviews with teachers, it quickly became clear that the main reason younger children were not included in the school council was that staff felt it was both impractical and difficult in terms of implementation. The main reason for this view seemed to be a perception that young children would not have the emotional or intellectual maturity to be able to comment on discussions about the school community. Given that this inquiry was to take place over a relatively short period of time, and that the school was primarily interested in us adopting a solution-focused approach, we decided to make an assumption. In a different sort of research process, we might have asked the question, 'Are young children capable of identifying and commenting on issues which affect their community?' We decided that it was not feasible to conduct an in-depth investigation into this question. Instead, we chose to assume that young children *are* capable of identifying and commenting on issues which affect their community and, having made this assumption, to focus our energies on finding means to enable them to do so.

After attending a school council meeting, we observed a number of factors that would be likely to pose barriers to the youngest children's participation. The fact that the way the school council meetings are run requires that members of the council speak up in front of the whole council could present a real difficulty for younger members. In the meeting we attended, we noticed that the children from Years 5 and 6 very much dominated the discussions, while the younger children were more reticent. Our observations led us to feel that it was quite intimidating for the existing members of the council to voice their views and that for very young children this could well be even more of an obstacle.

Meanwhile, our literature search revealed an argument which states that there has been a sociological shift in thinking about children. Children are no longer seen as 'adults-in-the-making' but rather as 'beings' whose views are important to hear (Clark *et al.*, 2003). This relatively recent development contradicts the long held view that children's opinions are not worth taking into account. This view regarding children's opinions seemed to us to have something of a legacy for the staff at Small Tree.

Our experience of the way the problem was framed in our early discussions showed that there was a feeling that the very young could not contribute, and yet this was combined with a clear sense that the school *should* be enabling them to contribute. So, perhaps, rather than young children not having opinions at all, it occurred to us that the problem may be that the structures which are in place for expression of views are not appropriate. The real issue at hand was emerging as the need to find a mechanism or means which would enable the very young to express their views. This led us to formulate the key question which underpinned our inquiry: *How can young children be enabled to comment on issues affecting their school experience?* With this focus clearly in mind, we set out to explore possible strategies.

The question of how to capture the voices of typically excluded groups was tackled within the school review instrument, *The Manchester Inclusion Standard*, which advocates an open minded and creative approach (Moore *et al.*, 2007). As we began our inquiry we felt particularly aware of this need for openness and creativity.

Opinion dice

First, we decided to adapt a technique described as *feeling dice* in *The Manchester Inclusion Standard* pupil-voice toolkit (Moore *et al.*, 2007: 83–84). The feeling dice is an elicitation tool designed to get children talking about events or circumstances and the particular emotions associated with these experiences. A specially made dice is given to the child to roll. When it lands, the child is asked to give an example of an experience which causes them to feel the feeling displayed on the dice.

We adapted this idea to come up with *opinion dice*. Rather than being interested in the individual child's emotional landscape, we were more interested in their attitudes and judgements about the school community. We made our own dice which displayed the following dimensions: SAFE, UNSAFE, UPSET, CROSS, HAPPY, SAD, with illustrations representing each of the descriptors. Working with groups of four children, we explained that we would like them to take it in turns rolling the dice, and then tell us about something which happens at school which might make them or some-one else feel that way. We trialled the opinion dice with six groups of four children, working for 10–15 minutes with two groups of four from each of the three year groups.

When we were working with children from the Nursery, we encountered some difficulties in getting the most out of the use of opinion dice. It seemed that the children enjoyed playing with the dice, but the conversations that accompanied the activity were not really related to their opinions on life at nursery. Our interpretation of their difficulty in responding was that they may have been unable to distinguish between the emotions depicted on each face of the dice. It may also have been the case that we did not frame the exercise in the most appropriate way for Nursery children. This experience gave us the feeling that if the very youngest children in the school *were* able to express their opinions, this technique was not the way to enable them to do so.

However, the children from Reception and Year 1 were significantly more capable of engaging in the activity and made some relevant comments. During the dice activity with one of the Year 1 groups, some useful com-ments were made. When the dice was rolled and landed on SAFE, one of the responses was 'I feel safe because there are rules – so people have to be good'.

On another occasion, the dice landed on UNSAFE and a child responded, 'I feel unsafe when someone is naughty in my class'.

Although the technique was more successful when used with Reception and Year 1 children, we came away feeling that using the dice did not really bring a magic ingredient to small group discussions, and that in some ways the dice was more of a distraction than an enabling tool. Overall, our feeling was that the opinion dice – certainly in the way that we implemented its use – was not an effective vehicle for eliciting views and opinions from younger children. It may have been simpler to have small group discussions structured around a series of quite simple questions.

Photo-elicitation

We then decided to try using photographs to stimulate conversations about issues of concern to the young children (Kaplan *et al.*, 2007). Having read about the use of this approach, we felt that it might enable younger children to communicate their opinions by presenting them with an image to focus on and discuss. In the first instance, we selected a range of subjects to photograph and created the images ourselves. We deliberately tried to capture the child's eye view, and took photographs within the early years' classrooms, as well as in the communal spaces throughout the school. The photographs were selected to reflect current themes on the school council agenda. At the same time, we chose to photograph other subjects which we felt may generate new issues of significance to the children.

Using these images, we conducted photo-elicitation interviews with groups of four children. We spoke to two groups of four from each of the early years' classes. We showed them one image at a time and asked them to tell us what they thought the image was about.

Our experience of using the activity with children from Reception and Year 1 was largely successful and rewarding. The children in these groups made interesting and relevant comments and suggestions when they saw the photographs, and lively discussion followed. The aim of the exercise was clear to them and they were good at expressing their opinion about school-related issues.

The photographs worked very effectively as a trigger to encourage children to talk about issues of concern to them and we felt that the matters which arose from the discussions were relevant and valuable to the school council. We concluded that the use of photographs in this way was much more successful than discussions stimulated by the use of opinion dice or simply having one-to-one conversations with the young people. Specifically, the concrete visual stimulus of the photographic image seemed to make it easy for children to comment and express their opinions about the way in which they experienced the school environment.

However, our experience of using photos to elicit responses from the Nursery children was rather different. Similar to the opinion dice activity, we again felt that the children in the Nursery found it difficult to respond in the way we hoped. While they seemed to enjoy looking at the photographs, their responses were largely descriptive rather than containing critical reflection on their school experience. During the discussions we also found that the Nursery children did not seem very able to listen to one another and reflect on the contributions and views of others in the group.

At this point in our investigations we began to feel that the techniques we were testing to encourage young children to express themselves were not really working with the Nursery-age children. This raised the question as to whether it was because we, as researchers, had not found the right technique, or whether, in fact, very young children were actually not developmentally mature enough to be able to think critically rather than just descriptively, or to comment on the circumstances of their community. It certainly seemed to be the case that the techniques we had tested were more effective and suitable for use with children from Reception and Year 1.

Ambassadors

A primary aim of our inquiry at Small Tree School was to offer practical techniques for enabling the very young to contribute to the council process. Our input was not going to be an ongoing or lasting resource for the school, so it was necessary to think of ways of sustaining the activity after we left.

Given that the photo-elicitation activity had been the most successful of the techniques we had tried, we thought about strategies for practically implementing this technique in a way which would allow it to be used to feed directly into the school council. Through discussion we came up with the idea of recruiting *ambassadors*, who would be older children from Year 6 at the school. The ambassadors' role would be to work individually with children from the early years' classes to find out their opinions and views on issues which were of current concern to the school council.

The ambassadors would take photographs which represented or symbolised a particular issue or concern. They would visit the young child in their classroom, and have a conversation with them about what the photograph meant to them. The ambassador would then be able to feed back to the rest of the school council what the younger child had said. In this way, the young children would have the opportunity to express a view, without the barrier of having to speak in front of a large group of people. It would also be an empowering and useful exercise for the ambassadors to be engaged in, and would interrupt the school's thinking about the school council.

We tested the technique and found there were great advantages to using this approach in order to elicit the views of younger children. First of all, there was a positive dynamic between the ambassadors and the younger children. The young children seemed to find it easier to talk to another child than they did when working with adult researchers. Second, the technique resulted in the young children making comments which were applicable and relevant to the remit of the school council.

The older children who acted as ambassadors reported that they enjoyed being given the responsibility. It was clear that they had thought seriously about the photographs they took and that they were far more pertinent than those we had taken ourselves. They said that they understood the purpose of the exercise and they took it very seriously and approached this task as a challenge. They were extremely adept at getting the younger children to talk about the photographs and encouraged them towards the most relevant agenda. One commented: 'They liked talking to us and we did get quite a lot of information.' Another added: 'We gave them a chance to say something and now we know what they want.'

Some examples of the photographs taken by ambassadors are shown below. The first shows basketball hoops in the playground (Figure 6.1). This led to a discussion about how the younger children felt it was unfair that they were excluded from playing in that part of the playground.

The second photograph (Figure 6.2) shows the computer room with egg timers next to the computers. This photograph stimulated discussion about how the children would like more opportunities to use this room.

Figure 6.1 Basketball court in juniors' playground – 'Why can't we have one?'

Figure 6.2 Computers with egg timers – 'We are only allowed a short time to work on the computers.'

They felt there should be more computers in their classroom, and also said that it was not fair that older children had freer access to the room and no time limit.

In the third photograph we can see a wash basin (Figure 6.3). The child who was shown this photograph commented that there was often no soap, which meant that they could not wash their hands properly.

We felt that photographs taken by the ambassadors were extremely relevant to the children who were interviewed about them, and that they certainly acted as a useful channel through which young children were enabled to express their opinions. The ambassadors were able to report back to the rest of the school council what the young children had said. For this reason, we concluded that this particular approach in using photo-elicitation techniques led by older children seemed to have the most practical application in the school – one which promotes positive relationships between pupils across year groups, while at the same time generating useful information for the inquiry.

Figure 6.3 Washbasin with no soap!

Final thoughts

The research we have described was a small attempt to look at an important issue for staff working with young children. In this sense, the techniques we have explored can be seen as starting points.

For us, working as consultants to Small Tree School was a great learning experience. The overall approach we used was that of action research, which meant that we *learnt by doing*. Having developed a research question that focused our inquiry, we actively explored the situation in the school, using systematic observation and informal interviews to evaluate the impact of the techniques we trialled. This led us to reflect upon our own experiences, together with our colleagues in the school, in order to draw out the lessons. Having said this, it is likely that a different team of researchers would have conducted this study in a different way, and that their conclusions could have contradicted ours.

Time constraints set limits on the action research we were able to carry out – as a result, we only trialled each technique twice. It may be that we would have found different results if we could have worked with more children, at different times of the day or week, and with more time to reflect upon the findings between the trials.

We think that more could be done to continue the research we have started. In particular, the idea of ambassadors is extremely promising, particularly where members of a school council take on the role. The first challenge, of course, would be to train the older pupils to work as researchers. It occurs to us that the dice game could be developed for their use. Similarly, the technique of *learning walks*, where small groups of children discuss aspects of the school as they go around the building commenting on their experiences, might be relevant. Clearly this technique needs research of the sort we carried out in order to determine its value.

Three years after our project, we hear that the ambassador structure is still being used in Small Tree Primary School. Apparently, members of the school council continue to talk to children in Nursery, Reception and Year 1 on a regular basis in order to take account of their ideas and changes they would like to see. The implication is that those in the school have recognised the power of evidence as a means of fostering more effective ways of involving young children in the development of their school.

References

Clark, A., McQuail, S. and Moss, P. (2003) *Exploring the Field of Listening to and Consulting with Young Children*. Research Report 445. London: Department for Education and Skills.

Kaplan, I., Lewis, I. and Mumba, P. (2007) 'Picturing global educational inclusion? Looking and thinking across students' photographs from the UK, Zambia and Indonesia'. *Journal of Research in Special Educational Needs*, 7(1): 23–35.

Moore, M., Ainscow, M. and Fox, S. (2007) *The Manchester Inclusion Standard*. Manchester: Manchester City Council.

Chapter 7

Involving young children in behaviour management strategies

A classroom-based inquiry

Pamela Aspin

This chapter tells the story of a small group of children who took on the responsibility of monitoring and modifying behaviour in their class with the support of their teacher and a visiting behaviour advisory teacher. A mixed group of five children between the ages of 6–7 years old were selected and the inquiry took place over a period of nine weeks. The children were taught the skills of *self-management* of pro-social classroom behaviours. The inquiry reported here sought to examine whether the students could learn to support *each other* to adhere to the social expectations of a busy classroom community, rather than relying on the teacher to assume sole control of behaviour management.

In this chapter I report my attempts to explore ways in which children can support one another in developing more appropriate classroom behaviour. The project developed from my day-to-day practice as a part-time behaviour advisory teacher. Through a collaborative action research partnership with a teacher in a primary school, I was able to explore new possibilities for developing her practice and my own.

Behaviour support

Over the past seven years I have worked as a member of the Inclusion Support Team, now known as the Emotional Well-being in Schools Team. At the time of the inquiry the team included educational psychologists, family support workers and behaviour advisory teachers. It has now expanded to include social workers and a Child and Adolescent Mental Health Support worker.

The main remit of the service is to reduce exclusions from mainstream primary and secondary schools, by supporting them to include young people who are at risk of exclusion for misbehaviour. My specific remit is to offer advice and strategies to class teachers in relation to children with challenging behaviour and in managing classroom behaviour in general.

In my experience, many teachers come to depend heavily on support staff due to the inherent stress involved in teaching while at the same time dealing with challenging behaviour. Subsequently, some teachers tend to believe that children who have challenging behaviour require specialist support and are not suited to mainstream education. In this way, the involvement of support staff can reduce the incentive to look for other strategies when difficulties arise. As Ainscow (1999, p. 63) suggests, the 'existence of support may eliminate the possibility that the demands of these individuals could stimulate a consideration of how practice might be changed in an attempt to facilitate their participation'.

Generally, a package of support is developed by the school and the behaviour advisory service, in partnership with the young person who is at risk of exclusion and their family. The outcome of a multi-agency meeting is normally the production of a Pastoral Support Plan, or an amended Individual Education Plan detailing what will be done in school and at home to avoid the imminent exclusion. As a result of this process, teachers may be advised to modify their behaviour management strategies or explore alternative teaching styles.

The successful implementation of the agreed plan can take considerable commitment from all stakeholders involved, over a significant period of time. The key person is arguably the class teacher, who has the most daily contact with the young person. It is my experience that there is more likelihood of success when the class teacher is genuine in their attempts to include the child in the class, even if it means changing *their* behaviour or changing the way the class is managed. When a teacher is unwilling to fully engage and commit to a planned intervention, then the child is more likely to be excluded.

In saying this, I do not mean to be judgemental of colleagues. I recognise that attempts to ensure the continued inclusion of a child with challenging behaviour takes a great deal of emotional and physical effort; both of which can be very demanding and demoralising on an already stressed and overworked teacher.

Prior to conducting this inquiry, I had come to the conclusion that those strategies designed to be employed by young people themselves tended to lead to the most positive results. I began to wonder whether a positive difference in the young person's behaviour from participating in these strategies gave the teacher an opportunity to view the young person in a new light. Therefore, in my advisory role, my response to teachers' negative attitudes to children's misbehaviour had developed as follows:

- If children have more control and ownership over the strategies employed to encourage pro-social classroom behaviour, they are more likely to change their behaviour in line with what is expected.

- Teachers need to share more of the responsibility of the smooth running of the class 'community' with all the stakeholders in that community, namely, the children.
- A more collaborative approach to behaviour management would help to reduce the stress involved in managing an average class of 30 children, some of whose behaviour disturbs the teaching and learning process.

The Department for Children, Schools and Families (DCSF) recently updated their guidance to schools on the issue of pupil voice and pupil participation (2008). These guidelines promote the participation of children and young people in decision-making in school. The DCSF argues that this can improve engagement in learning, help develop a more inclusive school environment and improve behaviour and attendance. The school inspection service, Ofsted, now has to consider the views of pupils when conducting routine inspections, and assesses the extent to which schools seek the views of pupils and take action in response to these views. The pupil participation agenda is further underpinned by the United Nations *Convention on the Rights of the Child* (1989) and the *Every Child Matters* policy (DCSF, 2004).

The 'A' team

My interest in exploring the idea of involving children in interventions to address challenging behaviour developed through my collaboration with a colleague who is an educational psychologist. His thinking had developed as a result of witnessing the positive impact that the 'Circle of Friends' technique (Newton *et al.*, 1996) had had on an individual with challenging behaviour. The approach we agreed to trial was rather similar. Known as the 'A' team, it adapted the ingredients from a variety of peer group interventions for the self-monitoring of pupil behaviour (Lloyd and Landrum, 1990; Hallahan *et al.*, 1981).

An 'A' team is a supportive group of peers who enable an individual to progress and resolve difficulties, while also developing skills useful to all children. This is achieved through mechanisms, such as:

- skill teaching, prompting and reinforcement
- task/rule clarification
- peer modelling
- emotional support (listening, being available) and problem solving.

I envisioned that if this intervention worked for one group in a class, then maybe it could be used as a whole class intervention. In this way, a group of individuals in the classroom community would become partly responsible for the behaviour of the whole. This initial inquiry was, in effect, a pilot study for a further case study which would look at the whole class.

This approach to behaviour modification is informed by theories of emotional literacy and emotional intelligence (Goleman, 1998). What interested me about the 'A' team idea was that it offered a group of children the opportunity to become 'mini behaviour managers' trained in the art of the language of discipline (Rogers, 2002), supporting, encouraging and maintaining the equilibrium of the classroom in partnership with the class teacher. There would be a shared responsibility for the smooth running of the classroom (Aspin, 2009).

Developing a research relationship

The choice of a school in which to conduct my inquiry was based on practical considerations – it was crucial that the visits to the school fitted in with my working day. It also made practical sense to choose a school with which I had developed a working relationship and one that had benefitted from the service that I provide.

The primary school that I chose will be referred to as Rosegrove. Altogether I had made eight previous visits to this school over the course of three years and, as a result, the staff were familiar with the type of work that I do. I felt confident that there would be a level of trust between us – a critical factor in conducting an exploratory inquiry.

During the previous year I had worked intensively with a teacher at Rosegrove who had requested support and guidance from our Inclusion Support Team. She needed guidance on developing strategies to deal with the management of a difficult Year 2 class. Together we devised a variety of whole class interventions that would help ease the challenging behaviour. These interventions were successful and the teacher was enthusiastic about sharing these ideas with other members of staff. This teacher was also working on her Master's degree at another university, and so could relate to the challenge I faced.

She announced the fact that I wanted to conduct an inquiry at a staff meeting, and a keen young teacher, who I will call Miss Green, volunteered to be involved. I had observed this teacher's class several months before and offered guidance, so we had already developed a working relationship.

Miss Green was enthusiastic and had a positive relationship with her pupils. She was keen to embrace new ideas, especially if they were linked to equipping her with strategies to help manage behaviour. When I explained the idea of the 'A' team project I had to make it clear that I was not coming in with my advisory hat on, but that I was coming in as a teacher who was also interested in finding out if the 'A' team had potential for wider use in other school contexts. Establishing the purpose of my inquiry was important, as I had initially sensed from the teacher that she was intimidated my advisory role.

I wanted to develop an equal working partnership, as far as possible, in order to develop the notion that we were working *together* on an action research project to improve both our practices – mine as an advisory teacher and hers as a classroom teacher. This was important if the teacher was to feel any ownership over the process and really become involved in the inquiry. I wanted to learn from Miss Green's experiences of the 'A' team and to have professional discussions about the impact that the 'A' team had on the teacher, the class and the group.

One strategy that I used to put Miss Green at ease was to discuss my teaching career with her, talking candidly about my experiences of children with challenging behaviour and how much of a challenge that it can be. Hopefully she would view me as human being and relate to me as a classroom teacher, not as just as an official from the local authority.

Managing the collaborative inquiry

My collaborative action research inquiry involved a process of planning, action, observation and reflection (Carr and Kemmis, 1986), focused on the following research question: *Can children help to promote pro-social classroom behaviours in the primary classroom?* Miss Green managed the intervention on a daily basis and recorded her observations and reflections in a diary, and we held weekly supervision meetings in her classroom after school. She rather reluctantly agreed to communicate with me through email – she was not familiar with electronic communication, but committed herself to learning how to use it since regular face-to-face discussions were not possible, neither was telephone communication. I felt it was important that we communicated regularly so that Miss Green did not feel abandoned, but felt part of a team. It was clear from the beginning that it was going to be a challenge!

In addition to the regular communication with Miss Green, I organised fortnightly supervision meetings with the 'A' team. We arranged these meetings after break time, so that Miss Green and I could have a few minutes during break time to discuss the inquiry. This was difficult as break time is a pressured time, during which the next lesson has to be set up and a well-earned cup of tea consumed! It was a delicate balancing act, but one that I think went well on the whole – possibly because I know from experience what it is like to be a class teacher.

I provided Miss Green with a strategic overview, as well as a week-by-week action plan describing how we would implement the inquiry. We put dates in our diaries for the various training sessions and supervision meetings which would take place, avoiding the various school activities that were scheduled for the summer term. This was a practical measure to enable us to see at a glance who should be doing what and when. This was an invaluable investment of time on my part as it enabled the process to run as smoothly as possible.

I drafted a letter to parents asking permission for their children to take part in the inquiry. The letter was important in addressing the ethical issues involved in conducting the inquiry, and in complying with the school's policy on communication with parents. I emailed the letter to both the teacher and the head teacher and awaited their approval. This also gave me the opportunity to make contact with the head teacher to explain the inquiry and make sure that she was happy with the research plan.

Getting going

Miss Green was in charge of choosing the group to become the 'A' team, since she knew the children. However, I stipulated that the group should include:

1   at least two good behaviour role models
2   one pupil who was working on an Individual Behaviour Plan.

My rationale in selecting role models was not unlike the strategy a class teacher may employ when allocating children to groups for routine activities.

Miss Green decided that it was best for her to make use of the 'A' team in the afternoons when the children were seated in mixed ability groups, since in the mornings they were seated according to their attainment in literacy and numeracy lessons. We agreed that the 'A' team would be used for one session each afternoon, and then the children would return to their usual mixed ability groups.

The 'A' team principle was first introduced to the five children by Miss Green. This was to reassure the children that she was part of the process and would be facilitating it, and give her the opportunity to explain the behaviour expectations. This enabled me to squeeze the 'A' team training into the short time available to me on my visit to the school.

The training involved teaching the children the roles of Job Finisher, Job Checker, Rule Reminder, Encourager and Target Buddy. Roles would rotate each week. The target child – who was working on the individual behaviour plan – would be included in this role allocation. Cue cards would be used to remind children of their roles, and to provide them with positive language with which to speak to each other. The wording on the cue cards would be developed by the children and the class teacher – in the light of real issues in the classroom context.

Before meeting the group on their own, I carried out an observation of the group members in the classroom, and paid particular attention to the target child who was working on an Individual Behaviour Plan. I also did a frequency count observation as a baseline assessment (which I will explain in more detail later). I then observed the group as a whole. Afterwards I arranged to meet the 'A' team in the library. However, the library had been booked, so I had to negotiate a space with the teacher using the library. This was a common occurrence – we often had to find a space in the hall or a corridor at the last minute.

In this first meeting, I had to gain credibility by ensuring that the children behaved well – any misbehaviour at this point could have jeopardised the inquiry and wasted valuable time. I began by explaining the rewards offered to 'A' team members, and went on to outline the respective 'A' team roles. The children had been asked to produce pictures of themselves which they used in a warm-up activity to introduce themselves.

Managing the group's behaviour in such a public way was, undoubtedly, an added pressure of conducting this inquiry in a school in which I was well known. I was, after all, the 'Behaviour Advisory Teacher' and was expected to do so with ease – yet, I had to send one of the children back to the class, as he was not taking the training very seriously.

Miss Green reported that the members of the 'A' team were a little excited at the beginning of the inquiry, as they were not used to working together and this was a new experience. Eventually, though, they settled into their new group with its specified roles. I observed this excitement at the beginning of the inquiry and made a note of it in my field notes. I was concerned that the group would not 'gel', but these initial problems gradually resolved themselves.

The intervention

I organised two hour-long sessions to train the team members in their respective roles, while at the same time ensuring that the whole team understood each other's roles, which were:

Job Checker: To check that individuals and group know what they're doing – checks with teacher if necessary.
Rule Reminder: To remind group of selected classroom rules, if they are being infringed.
Encourager: To notice when the group is working well and make encouraging comments to all members, including the target child.
Target Buddy: To support the target child with their behaviour target.
Job Finisher: To give reminders of the task and the time left, and ensure that the group continues working and does not go off-task.

For each role there was a role card with an example of what they might say to a member of the group. For example:

RULE REMINDER

Your job is to remind the group about three classroom rules. They are:
'Put your hand up to ask questions.'
'Stay in your place unless Miss says.'
'Talk in your partner voice only.'

We used role play to practise the roles, although the time allocated for this was too short – the children had to miss lessons and my time was also restricted. The remainder of the training, therefore, had to be 'on the job'. In addition, the children had cue cards for each role to help them reinforce positive, pro-social behaviour. The group used the fledgling skills learnt in the two sessions and applied them in real-life situations with myself observing and facilitating the group. This refining of skills continued under Miss Green's supervision, and I was able to use excerpts from Miss Green's diary to structure my supervision meetings with the 'A' team.

Meanwhile, I decided to meet the target child on his own, and then together with the Target Buddy. I felt that it was ethically correct to ensure that the Target Child was happy with the process being put forward and that he had the opportunity to ask questions. I then introduced him to his target buddy since they were not friends in class. It was important to explain that, although the target child had his own role in the 'A' team (e.g. Encourager), the introduction of a Target Buddy was a strategy that would be added to his Individual Behaviour Plan to help him achieve his target of 'staying on task during independent activities with 90 per cent success'. The meeting was also to ensure that the Target Buddy understood what was expected and to explain that it was a very special role. After each supervision meeting I had private discussions with both the Target Buddy and the target child as this allowed me to ensure that the issues relating to the target child were discussed with dignity.

Analysing the process

Once I had completed the training, Miss Green was essentially in charge of the day-to-day running of the inquiry. The expectations were that she would:

- inform the team members when the 'A' team is 'on duty';
- set the team a target number of pieces of work to complete for that week;
- keep a record of how many tasks have been completed on a log sheet;
- praise the group for successfully carrying out roles and model the correct use of the roles;
- reward the group with the rewards negotiated with them;
- praise the target child for meeting his behaviour targets;
- document observations of the group during 'A' team time in a diary.

It was then my responsibility to conduct weekly supervision meetings to:

- organise role swaps for the following week;
- provide the team with praise for their successes – using the teacher's diary and the reward log sheet;

- provide further training on areas identified by the teacher or as a result of my regular observations;
- monitor task completion, based on feedback from the teacher.

The methods I used to monitor the process were: participant observation of the 'A' team members within their class; semi-structured interviews with the teacher and the children; a teacher's research diary; my own research diary; informal chats; and a questionnaire administered to the children.

Miss Green agreed to keep a diary to document her observations of the group when they were 'working' in the 'A' team. Initially I decided not to be too prescriptive with what I wanted in the diary, as I felt that this was a personal process. At one stage I noted in my own research diary:

> The diary entries from the teacher were mainly about her observations about the group and not so much about her thoughts and feelings regarding the process. I guess I was not very clear about the diary as I'm not sure what the focus should be – therefore have left it to the discretion of the teacher.

I did not want her to be trying to record what she thought I wanted, when all I wanted was her own natural responses to what she observed. I was so very grateful that Miss Green was willing to find the time to write anything at all, that I did not feel that I should make particular demands.

As the weeks passed and I read her diary entries during my supervision meetings, I was very impressed with the amount of information that she was collecting. However, I felt that I needed to know more about her feelings about what she was observing in order to obtain data related to my research question. I mentioned this to Miss Green, and the following week's diary entries reflected on the 'A' team process and the impact that it had on her. I was really glad that I had made these comments!

I was also keen to investigate the impact of the 'A' team in improving the on-task behaviour of the target child, so I completed a frequency count of his on-task/off-task episodes. I did this by placing myself in the classroom in a position where I was unobtrusive to the group. The teacher assured me that the children were used to having adults in the room due to Ofsted and internal lesson observations.

Using a tape recorder with beeps that sounded at 10-second intervals, I observed the target child and noted down whether he was on- or off-task. I also made a note of anything of interest in the context at the time. I tried to hide the tape recorder from the group to avoid the children becoming curious about me and so becoming distracted from their work. I repeated this frequency count during my last observation, however, this time the target child knew I was in the classroom to observe the group. Ideally, I would have collected such data over a longer period of time as the frequency log did not produce helpful results as part of this inquiry.

Alongside the research diaries and observations I carried out, I also kept field notes. These were a valuable tool to use for triangulation, as I could compare my observations with the teacher's diary. They were useful, too, in highlighting interesting events that I wished to bring to the teacher's attention through the diaries and modifications to the 'A' team during the process.

However, field notes are best written as close to the event as possible and most of the time I was not able to write my notes until I had some spare time, usually many hours or even days later. This is one of the difficulties in conducting an inquiry while still involved in a professional role. In addition, I had a young child at home and my second baby was born just weeks after I finished collecting my data – I returned to the data analysis following my maternity leave.

Further data were collected through a survey and informal discussions with children. I designed a questionnaire with the age and ability of the pupils in mind. I wanted the questionnaire to look appealing, and so I gave them a choice of three bright yellow faces (smile, frown and neutral) to give their responses to the straightforward questions. I also included more searching questions which required them to reflect on their experience and express their opinions. I offered to scribe the answers for those children who did not wish to write in front of me – I wanted the pupil to concentrate on the answer and not become worried about spelling or handwriting.

I made the decision to talk to each pupil individually to evaluate the 'A' team initiative. From my previous experience with the group, I was worried that some members may jeopardise the smooth running of a focus group, and that some of the quieter members may not have been heard. In the individual 'interviews' I tried to put each child at ease, explaining that there were no right or wrong answers, and that I was very interested in what they had to tell me about the 'A' team. I explained that I had never done this before, and as I was not in the class all of the time, I needed them to help me.

The children made many revealing comments about the process. One particularly enlightened comment involved a reflection about being the Target Buddy:

> people would get on to me telling me to tell him off – but I'd rather tell him *for doing the right thing* rather than tell him off.
>
> (Aspin, 2009: 54)

Miss Green and I felt that this comment revealed great insight into positive behaviour management – insight that was arguably 'beyond the child's years'. Yet, this group of 6 year olds had demonstrated that they were capable of assuming considerable responsibility. In the previous chapter, staff questioned the ability of children of the same age to participate in the school council.

Both of these chapters demonstrate that young children are capable of a great deal more than is often realised, and that they are, therefore, an underused resource in our schools.

Final reflections

> In the A team we have been making sure people are ok and have been encouraging people, like saying 'well done', or telling them to get on with their work.
>
> (child interview)

The children in this study were capable of correcting each other's behaviour, helping with work, timekeeping and praising efforts. They enjoyed encouraging each other and having peer support in class. However, the extent to which the correcting of behaviour was respectfully conducted and the praising of behaviour carried out without prompting is questionable. Nevertheless, the children certainly appeared to find that *correcting* behaviour came naturally. They did this with some structure, careful guidance and monitoring, and demonstrated that, in partnership with their teacher, they had the necessary experience, and gained the appropriate skills, to manage their own work in a responsible way.

The children were highly motivated by the reward structure created for the 'A' team. However, they reported that they had also gained intrinsic enjoyment, saying they had enjoyed working in a team. Some children rose to the challenge of their particular role and said they liked 'telling other people in the group how much time we had left'. While others appreciated the structure it brought to their work: 'I liked it when we all went to our groups and started working quietly' (Aspin, 2009: 59).

It would be unethical to use the 'A' team as a method to create 'model' children who assist the teacher to maintain the status quo. An 'A' team should be guided in determining what is meant by *expected* behaviours. There is a danger that children could be encouraged to spend most of their day being quiet, docile and obedient 'young adults' (Winnet and Winkler 1972). This method does not involve encouraging children to be quiet or passive. The 'A' team method should only be used in the context of well-planned, quality lessons taught within a well-managed, secure and stimulating environment, where all children have the opportunity to be involved in the development of the class code of conduct and have their views heard, for example, through Circle Time.

Miss Green found the 'A' team inquiry to be a formative experience and said she would recommend the approach to her colleagues. In particular, she reported:

It has given me new ideas about how to develop independent learning instead of me constantly having to repeat the rules . . . I would certainly consider doing this next year but probably introduce it at the beginning of the year.

(Aspin, 2009: 61)

Working in partnership with a teacher, the children in this inquiry were enabled to take a more active role in influencing their own and their peers' pro-social classroom behaviours. The approach can reinforce pro-social behaviour, as well as enable children to access increased support with their work. However, children need time to practise the 'A' team skills and learn from the behaviour that is being modelled by teachers and support staff. On some occasions, I observed that the children had forgotten to correct behaviour in a respectful manner. This is a social skill learnt from adults and it has implications for the adults' behaviour in the classroom. The adults would have to think far more carefully about how they interact with the pupils in their class as pupils are being actively encouraged to emulate this behaviour in order to respectfully share responsibility for the development of more positive behaviour in classroom communities.

A postscript

My educational psychologist colleague offered the following reflections on the origin of the 'A' team idea presented in this chapter:

An influential book about emotional intelligence (Chapman, 2001) suggests that, as adults, we should build a supportive group (or A Team) around us, of people who can offer different sorts of support: people who will listen, people who will validate us and those upon whom we can depend in a crisis. This led me to wonder what a supportive group around a child might look like. What about developing support groups for the core business of the classroom?

Other interests also contributed to my thinking: social skills training and encouraging children to take greater responsibility for self-management; social learning theory and its emphasis on role modelling; ways of embedding rules, routines and positive behaviour in the busy world of the primary classroom.

My idea was to identify a set of key skills that, hypothetically, should contribute to group functioning in the classroom, and what roles and systems could promote those skills. Task completion, rule reinforcement, and problem-solving emerged as key areas for development and these were twinned with providing a special ally, or prompt, for a child with particular difficulties. A Teams for primary-aged children started to take shape in the mist.

However, ideas need skilled practitioners to turn them into reality, and A Teams might still be gathering static on my hard drive had Pamela Aspin not seen their potential. I am grateful for her vision, energy and attention to detail; it is these that have developed the original idea into something that may prove to be genuinely useful to classroom practitioners.

References

Ainscow, M. (1999) *Understanding the Development of Inclusive Schools*. London: Falmer.

Aspin, P. (2009) *Child Participation in Classroom Behaviour Management: A Case Study*. Unpublished Master's dissertation. Manchester: University of Manchester.

Carr, W. and Kemmis, S. (1986) *Becoming Critical: Knowing Through Action Research*. London: Falmer.

Chapman, M. (2001) *The Emotional Intelligence Pocketbook*. Alresford: Management Pocketbooks.

Department for Children, Schools and Families (DCSF) (2004) *Every Child Matters: Change for Children*. London: DCSF. Available online at: http://www.dcsf.gov.uk/everychildmatters. Accessed 15 January 2009.

Department for Children, Schools and Families (DCSF) (2008) *Working Together: Listening to the Voices of Children and Young People*. London: DCSF.

Goleman, D. (1998) *Working with Emotional Intelligence*. New York: Bantam Books.

Hallahan, D. P., Marshall, K. J. and Lloyd, J. W. (1981) 'Self recording during group instruction: effects on attention to task'. *Learning Disability Quarterly*, 4, 407–413.

Lloyd, J. W. and Landrum, T. J. (1990) 'Self recording of attention to task: treatment components and generalization of effects'. In T. E Scruggs and B. Y. L. Wong (eds) *Intervention Research in Learning Disabilities*. New York: Springer-Verlag, pp. 235–262.

Newton, C., Taylor, G. and Wilson, D. (1996) 'Circles of friends: an inclusive approach to meeting emotional and behavioral difficulties'. *Educational Psychology in Practice*, 11, 41–48.

Rogers, B. (2002) *Classroom Behaviour: A Practical Guide to Effective Teaching, Behaviour Management and Colleague Support*. London: Sage.

United Nations (1989) *Convention on the Rights of the Child*. New York: United Nations.

Winnett, R. A. and Winkler, R. C. (1972) 'Current behavior modification in the classroom: be still, be quiet, be docile'. *Journal of Applied Behavior Analysis*, 4, 499–504.

Chapter 8

Using the views of students to rethink

A collaborative inquiry in a further education college

Hannah Scott[1]

This chapter tells how students with learning difficulties and members of staff in a further education college in the north of England engaged in a critical collaborative inquiry with the support of an external researcher. The inquiry took place over the course of an academic year and was aimed at exploring ways in which students with learning difficulties might be more actively included and so empowered in their own learning. It was designed in response to the *inclusive learning* and *student voice* agendas within the further education sector.

The purpose of the study described in this chapter was to determine an effective means of eliciting responses from students with learning difficulties in a further education college about their preferred ways of learning. It also aimed to raise the students' educational status and encourage practitioners to reflect critically on their assumptions about the students.

The overall approach I used was that of collaborative inquiry. My intention was that this would act as a catalyst, bringing together both students and staff to review current educational provision. The specific research methods I explored included: body collages based upon the theory of *multiple intelligences* (Gardner, 1993), photo voice, reflective journals, student portfolios and interviews (see Table 8.1 for further details). Students and staff engaged in research training and cycles of reflection, where findings were discussed together with ways of implementing the learning from the inquiry process.

The inquiry aimed to minimise the gap that can be created through the professional-practitioner hierarchy, by providing an open forum where students could become consultants of their own learning. Staff members were also given the opportunity to explore their own practice through engaging with the students in this new way, and implementing what they learnt about each individual student.

As I show, this exploratory inquiry was successful, to some extent at least, in alerting staff to the benefits of listening to the voices of marginalised learners, such as those defined as having learning difficulties. It also generated some interesting findings about the co-operative experience, student self-reflective skills, their individual learning preferences and staff reflections.

The context for the study

I am a practitioner-researcher, engaged in doctoral research while also teaching part-time at a further education (FE) college for the past four years. I teach on a specialised vocational course, Skills for Independence, for young adults (aged 19–25) described as having severe learning difficulties. The course focuses upon practical activities, accessing the local community and developing communication and work-related skills. The aim of the course is to support students in developing greater autonomy, providing opportunities for them to speak up for themselves and carry out tasks independently, and enabling them to make key decisions about their lives as they approach the pivotal stage of transition into work. In this account I use the term *students with learning difficulties*, as this is preferred by the UK self-advocacy movement (Walmsley and Johnson, 2003), although it is acknowledged that *people with learning disabilities* is the official term used in the *Disability Discrimination Act* (HMSO, 1995).

Over recent years it has become increasingly apparent that the government is eager to encourage more inclusive practices in order to respond to student diversity in the FE sector (i.e. DfES, 2006). There has also been encouragement to develop personalised approaches within education and to cultivate democratic values through student-voice initiatives. To assist FE providers in incorporating these policies into practice, the Learning and Skills Council (LSC), (2007) produced a handbook, *Developing a Learner Involvement Strategy*. It states, 'Learner involvement covers a wide variety of practices that seek to enable, equip and motivate learners to voice their views and actively shape their learning' (p. 6). Although this provides a framework and poses questions to be considered about possible ways forward, the strategy encourages institutional discretion.

No matter how learner views are to be elicited, the LSC emphasises the need for a coordinated approach, thus encouraging practitioners to rise to the challenge of tackling educational barriers, driving improvements through direct consultations with students.

Such initiatives stem from the debate that developing democratic communities within educational contexts is an exploratory process that has to be practised. This calls for educators to create opportunities whereby students can become agents of change, making fundamental decisions and having a larger stake in their own learning. Such a process of engagement is referred to by Rudduck and Flutter (2000, p. 84) as 'a communal venturing forth' (quoting Aoki [1984]). In cultivating such approaches, where students and staff feel comfortable working together to review provision and make necessary changes, there is an expectation that they will evoke change and transcend beyond formal education.

Perspectives

Given that I had a central role in the study, it is important for readers to have a sense of the perspectives I brought to the task. Broadly, I adopted a *social model* perspective, which is concerned with addressing *barriers* in educational contexts and in society – both physical and attitudinal. Disabled activists have argued that by removing such barriers, impaired individuals would no longer feel discriminated and oppressed by society. For example:

> It is society [that] disables people with impairments and therefore any meaningful solution must be directed at societal change rather than the individual adjustment and rehabilitation.
>
> (Barnes *et al.*, 1999, p. 27)

Viewed through an educational lens, this entails looking critically at the learning environment and seeking more emancipatory opportunities for so-called learning-disabled students, rather than defining and grouping them into deficit learning categories. At the same time, it implies that such students should be empowered by giving them more of a say in their own learning and by exploring (disabling) perceptions of students by practitioners.

As I explained, I chose to use participatory orientation, along the lines of what has been defined as *collaborative inquiry* (Reason and Rowan, 1980; Reason, 1988). The use of such approaches emphasises the value of group processes and the use of varied methods of recording. In this way, I was eager to examine three overlapping themes: 1) what students advocate in relation to their own learning; 2) the challenges associated with such an inquiry; and 3) staff perceptions and attitudes about the students in terms of their educational status.

It has been argued that the voice of students is so seldom heard that there is often what seems like a 'culture of silence' (Gibson, 2006; Whitehurst, 2006). Others have argued that the ideals of inclusive education are unlikely to succeed unless young people are recognised for their individual contributions and are fully involved in the debate about educational purposes and processes (e.g. Shevlin and Rose, 2003; Gibson, 2006; Whitehurst, 2006). In an attempt to respond to such arguments, the Learning and Skills Development Agency (2006) produced guidance entitled *Nothing about Me, without Me: Involving Learners with Learning Difficulties or Disabilities*. These guidelines show examples of how students might be directly involved in projects through accessible methods, and influence the quality of their own provision. They were produced in the light of the *Disability Discrimination Act* (HMSO, 1995, 2005), part 4. New duties were enforced in FE from 2002 onwards, and the following 2005 *Disability Discrimination Act* (HMSO), rather than as a result of arguments for democratic reforms as advocated, for example, by Fielding (2001) and Rudduck and Fielding (2006).

In 2007, the Learning and Skills Research Council produced further guidelines, *Being, Having and Doing*, to aid practitioners in personalising educational support for students with learning difficulties, in which they advocate that students should be at the centre of the learning process, this being tailored according to their needs and aspirations. Such recommendations seem to imply a shift in the balance of power between students and practitioners, by enabling them to have a greater say in the planning and design of their own learning.

My own view is that such initiatives, while undoubtedly being a positive move, are unlikely to empower students if they fail to encourage educators to question their own attitudes towards students. Furthermore, my impression is that they have had little impact on practice in the field. Indeed, there is still ambiguity and confusion about how to implement personalised approaches and how to promote student voice in a meaningful way. More specifically, my impression is that many in the FE sector have embraced the rhetoric of inclusive ideals without understanding and addressing disabling standpoints and practices. As a result, practitioners are left feeling perplexed about their responsibilities and tend to become tokenistic in their desperation to adhere to external guidelines and institutional pressures to be seen to be taking account of their recommendations.

Since practitioners understand their own working environments, including the resources and support systems available and how best to utilise them, a bottom-up approach would be more effective. Tackling educational barriers, then, is about more than just addressing environmental factors by providing forums and accessible methods for students to voice opinions and share insights about themselves. Rather, it should involve giving practitioners spaces in which to reflect critically upon their own assumptions, while at the same time engaging in collaborative action. Consequently, there is a need to examine how student voices might be heard, in addition to acknowledging the tensions and complexities of such a process in action (Shevlin and Rose, 2003; Gibson, 2006; Whitehurst, 2006; Ravet, 2007).

Developing the co-operative approach

I focused upon critical participatory action research methodologies as a tool for improving lives and, more specifically, the educational experiences of students with learning difficulties. Empowering research of this nature should be a driving force through which students are given greater opportunities to participate, and be emancipated, through self-advocacy initiatives. In this way students can become co-researchers of their own learning, described by Walmsley and Johnson (2003) as *inclusive research* (see also Zarb [1992]).

Therefore, students' views about their individual provision should be directly represented in research findings and in their own words.

Such an exploration requires the use of innovative research methods that reach beyond the traditional notions of conducting an inquiry (Chappell *et al.*, 2001). Methods conducive to this particular methodology must be made accessible through the use of plain language, bullet points, symbols, photographs, illustrations and audio/video aids (Walmsley, 2001; Walmsley and Johnson, 2003).

Although inclusive research (as conducted through co-operative inquiries) has the potential to capture marginalised voices, as evident through independent advocacy groups (see, for example, Townson *et al.* [2004, 2007] and Wyre Forest Self Advocacy and Tarleton [2005]), there are few examples to illustrate how it might be directly applied in a classroom setting.

From these theoretical underpinnings I developed a co-operative framework (Heron and Reason's [2001]) and invited my colleagues and students at the college to participate. At the same time, I informed them that it would form part of my PhD research. The inquiry began in September 2008 and was completed by June 2009. There were ten co-researchers: five student co-researchers and four staff co-researchers, and myself, a practitioner-(co)researcher.

During the early stages of the inquiry, I hosted several introductory meetings to discuss the principles and practice of being co-researchers. I introduced the social model of disability and multiple intelligences theory, which we talked about at length. I also discussed different methods that would feature in our inquiry (body collages, portfolios, etc.), and invited the students to practice their interviewing skills, as well as exploring issues around ethics and how we could conduct research that would be respectful to everyone involved. Shortly after these preliminary meetings, I introduced the concept of researcher roles with staff assisting me in elaborating upon the different responsibilities assigned to each role. This was openly discussed, and staff and students opted for the roles in which they felt most comfortable.

It was mutually agreed that student researchers Frank and Shaffia would chair all our reflective meetings, in addition to interviewing other students and staff. James and Lee, also student researchers, wanted to be in charge of filming and taking photographs during our meetings. Kavita, a student researcher, was responsible for all our files, reflective journals and portfolios, ensuring everyone had their work when they needed it. Lorraine, a tutor, took the minutes for our meetings and Claudine, Tracey and Mark, support staff, assisted the students as required, usually with reading aloud, filming and downloading pictures onto the computer. My role was to facilitate the inquiry process by linking team members with each other and acting as a bridge between the team and the university and other research communities. This was quite a significant stage in the inquiry, as it marked the transition from my holding all the power to passing it onto the group, so that we could establish ourselves as a co-operative.

We then engaged in action by exploring innovative research methods, such as photo voice. The aim was to encourage self-reflection and group discussion about students' learning preferences. The methods used and findings presented in Table 8.1 have been adapted from one of our earlier publications (Ahmed *et al.*, 2009).

Table 8.1 Methods employed and critical reflections

Methods	Reflection on the process
Observations: I observed the students and made notes about how they were learning.	This initial phase enabled me to begin the process of exploration, as I adapted my practitioner role to that of a practitioner-(co)-researcher. Essentially, these findings forged the way for the students to be placed at the centre of the inquiry, as they shaped the interview questions and further discussions.
Body collages: The students drew around each other on large sheets of paper and placed a picture of themselves at the top (where their face would be). They were then given a selection of images, depicting the eight different intelligences, and asked to stick on the images that they felt best represented them as learners. They then presented their collages to the rest of the group, which led to further dialogue (see Figure 8.1).	Students found the body collage activity easier after we had adapted it slightly by creating two identical sets of pictures – one with blue borders representing activities they found easy or liked; the other with red borders for dislikes and activities they found difficult. This helped them reflect better on why they had chosen certain images, which also helped staff to understand them better.
Portfolios: Students collected examples of their work and pictures throughout the year. These showed them engaged in different college activities that they enjoyed and represented their strengths.	Body collages, portfolios and photo voice were deemed the most accessible activities, and most effective at eliciting responses. They enabled the students to control the research process, with little to no help from staff.
Photo voice: Photographs were taken by the students around the college that related to the college as a learning environment and aspirations the students had for the future.	

(continued on next page)

Table 8.1 (continued)

Methods	Reflection on the process
Reflective journal: Students recorded activities they liked doing by writing and collecting pictures. Staff recorded observations about individual students and personal reflections about their own teaching and supportive practice.	Students found it difficult to keep a reflective journal and/or to remember to fill it in. Staff, likewise, struggled to maintain their journals due to other work demands. However, they stated that there did need to be time set aside for critical reflection and thought weekly meetings with each other would be more ideal.
Interviews: Students interviewed each other based upon information gathered from the observations and body collages.	Students found some of the interview questions a bit confusing and so could not answer all of them.
Co-operative meetings: We met as a team to discuss what we had learned about the five students through the above activities, what actions the staff should take to meet individual learning needs and the students' aims after leaving college. We agreed on actions, and used similar activities to follow up on our progress (see Figure 8.2).	Conversations were open, with everyone contributing (through talking, filming, handing out information, etc.). All the students and staff went away with a clear idea of what needed to be done.

Figure 8.1 Frank placing his chosen images onto his body collage.

Figure 8.2 Co-operative meeting to prepare for end of year student presentations.

Drawing out the lessons

Each student was given the opportunity to share their educational preferences and have the responsibility of being a researcher. This led to a greater
understanding of each student as an individual. The students exercised their
skills in self-reflection, a process with which they struggled during the initial
stages. However, as the inquiry unfolded, the students became more self-
aware, growing in confidence in explaining their reasons for their preferences
in ever increasing detail.

Given that all of these young people were seen to have considerable difficulties in communicating their ideas, this was an outcome that was seen by
staff members as being very significant. They commented on how students
had become more vocal, volunteering information about themselves and not
being afraid to air their opinions to the rest of the group and other communities (when we exhibited our work outside of college). For example, Lee
rarely communicated verbally before the inquiry because he felt he was not
listened to. This emerged during the first body collage and interview. Now
he is much more willing to speak out and share his concerns.

We used college time to examine our findings and ensure everyone contributed to the discussion. During our first few meetings, staff tended to direct
the dialogue, with little input from students. It was only when our researcher
roles became defined that these power imbalances began to shift, making us
more equal as co-researchers, as we increasingly shared responsibility for
our findings.

Without our collaborative and individual commitment we would not have reached this far. Although collaborative inquires are considered useful enterprises for independent advocacy groups, they can present difficulties within educational settings. Despite difficulties associated with power relationships and time commitments, a co-operative approach enables everyone to come together, giving the student more responsibility and staff opportunity to critically reflect. This is particularly pertinent for FE provision, where students are young adults, and should be given more control over their own provision and in developing and exerting their self-reflective skills.

Staff were initially unsure as to what their responsibilities would involve at the start of the inquiry, which tended to result in them resuming authority over the students. However, once we assigned our differentiated roles, staff began to facilitate rather than dominate proceedings. Rather than questioning staff from the beginning about their perceptions and attitudes about the students, opportunities for them to critically reflect were subtly interwoven throughout. Consequently, it was only at the end of the research that their opinions were sought about the students as learners.

The process itself was challenging to all the participants, as new ideas and unexpected contributions created interruptions and forced individuals to reconsider their assumptions. This required us all to invest a substantial amount of time and energy.

Extracts taken from interviews carried out by Frank and Shaffia with staff members in relation to what they felt they had learnt about the students from doing the collaborative inquiry give a flavour of the impact:

> I might think you're good at something and you might think differently, I've learnt in that way, I've learnt more about you all . . . also you're taking pictures around college, I learnt a lot from that, because I would have given different answers about you, but it's not about me giving answers it's about you giving answers, so I learnt from that.

> I've learnt that there's more to you than meets the eye. I think in college we sometimes just scratch the surface of things, but I think it's been a good vehicle, a good method at finding out more about you and not what we think you need. It's something that we should continue.

Similarly, a member of staff commented to me about how her perceptions of the students had changed:

> I look at them more as an equal now and not as someone with a disability . . . I think, well they are intelligent, you've got to give them time and chance.

When talking about a particular student, she also commented:

He's not disabled is he? That's what we're looking at really, that's what made me look differently now . . . Even though I've worked here ten years, you do label students, well, I did do, thinking the students are disabled and, but now I don't look at it like that.

Some concluding thoughts

Student views need to serve the interests of those involved. As I have argued, learning about students individually fits well with notions of personalised learning – something that is increasingly at the heart of educational policy. And, as we have seen, it *is* possible for students described as having learning difficulties to become consultants on their own learning

I would argue that there has been too much attention placed on the physical attributes of a disabling environment, and not enough on attitudinal barriers, to the extent that these have been overlooked. By continuing in this way we are in danger of being lulled into a false sense of 'inclusive' security. In his participatory photography project with marginalised students, Kaplan (2008) asserts that it is easier for school staff to remedy problems noticeable in public spaces, rather than to reflect critically upon the inquiry process itself and the messages behind the pictures taken.

For these reasons, I argue that educators need to create co-operative spaces where students can voice ideas about themselves, have these learning preferences heard and invite practitioners to question assumptions. As we have seen, this involves a set of reflective processes that encourage ownership, empowerment and interruptions by what Ainscow (2007) and Delamont (1992) refer to as *making the familiar unfamiliar*.

I conclude, therefore, by reiterating that FE practitioners require more than just guidelines. Rather, they need tangible examples to support them in exploring and examining their own practices. I believe that it is only when the different components of, and spaces for, student voice, personalisation and critical reflection come together that genuine inclusive provision can be developed for students with learning difficulties and, indeed, other marginalised learners.

Note

1 I would like to acknowledge my fellow co-researchers (in alphabetical order): Shaffia Ahmed, Mark Atherton, Tracey Burns, Frank Lee, Kavita Lunj, Lee Noonan, Lorraine Pugh, James Ward and Claudine Willis.

References

Ahmed, S., Atherton, M., Burns, T., Lee, F., Lunj, K., Noonan, L., Pugh, L., Scott, H., Ward, J. and Willis, C. (2009) 'Learning disability and student voice in England'.

Enabling Education Network Newsletter. 13: 8. Manchester: Enabling Education Network (EENET).

Ainscow, M. (2007) 'Taking an inclusive turn'. *Journal of Research in Special Educational Needs.* 7(1): 3–7.

Aoki, T. (1984) 'Towards a reconceptualisation of curriculum implementation'. In D. Hopkins and M. Wideen (eds), *Alternative Perspectives on School Improvement.* London: Falmer.

Barnes, C., Mercer, G. and Shakespeare, T. (1999) *Exploring Disability: A Sociological Introduction.* Cambridge: Polity Press.

Chappell, A. L., Goodley, D. and Lawthorn, R. (2001) 'Making connections: the relevance of the social model of disability for people with learning difficulties'. *British Journal of Learning Disabilities.* 29(24): 45–50.

Delamont, S. (1992) *Fieldwork in Educational Settings: Methods, Pitfalls and Perspectives.* London: Falmer.

Department for Education and Skills (DfES) (2006) *Further Education: Raising Skills, Improving Life Chances.* White Paper, Cm 6768. Norwich: The Stationary Office (TSO).

Fielding, M. (2001) 'Students as radical agents of change'. *Journal of Educational Change.* 2: 123–141.

Gardner, H. (1993) *Multiple Intelligences: The Theory in Practice.* New York: Basic Books.

Gibson, S. (2006) 'Beyond the "culture of silence": inclusive education and the liberation of "voice"'. *Disability and Society.* 21(4): 315–329.

Her Majesty's Stationery Office (HMSO) (1995) *Disability Discrimination Act.* London: HMSO.

Her Majesty's Stationery Office (HMSO) (2005) *Disability Discrimination Act.* London: HMSO.

Heron, J. and Reason, P. (2001) 'The practice of co-operative inquiry: research "with" rather "on" people'. In P. Reason and H. Bradbury (eds) *Handbook of Action Research: Participative Inquiry and Practice.* London: Sage, pp. 179–188.

Kaplan, I. (2008) 'Being "seen" being "heard": engaging with students on the margins of education through participatory photography'. In Thomson, P. (ed.) *Doing Visual Research with Children and Young People.* London: Routledge, pp. 175–191.

Learning and Skills Council (LSC) (2007) *Developing a Learner Involvement Strategy: A Handbook for the Further Education Sector.* Coventry: LSC.

Learning and Skills Development Agency (2006) *Nothing About Me, Without Me: Involving Learners with Learning Difficulties or Disabilities.* London: Learning and Skills Network.

Learning and Skills Research Centre (2007) *Being, Having and Doing: Theories of Learning and Adults with Learning Difficulties.* London: Learning and Skills Network.

Reason, P. (1988) *Human Inquiry in Action: Developments in New Paradigm Research.* London: Sage.

Reason, P. and Rowan, J. (1980) *Human Inquiry: A Sourcebook of New Paradigm Research.* Oxford: John Wiley & Sons.

Ravet, J. (2007) 'Enabling pupil participation in a study of perceptions of disengagement: methodological matters'. *British Journal of Special Education.* 34(4): 234–242.

Rudduck, J. and Fielding, M. (2006) 'Student voice and the perils of popularity'. *Educational Review.* 58(2): 219–231.

Rudduck, J. and Flutter, J. (2000) 'Pupil participation and pupil perspective: "carving a new order of experience"'. *Cambridge Journal of Education.* 30(1): 75–89.

Shevlin, M. and Rose, R. (2003) *Encouraging Voices: Respecting the Insights of Young People Who Have Been Marginalised.* Dublin: National Disability Authority.

Townson, L., Macauley, S., Harkness, E., Chapman, R., Docherty, A., Dias, J., Eardley, M. and McNulty, N. (2004) 'We are all in the same boat: doing "people-led research"'. *British Journal of Learning Disabilities.* 32: 72–76.

Townson, L., Macauley, S., Harkness, E., Docherty, A., Dias, J., Eardley, M. and Chapman, R. (2007) 'Research project on advocacy and autism'. *British Journal of Learning Disabilities.* 22(5): 72–76.

Walmsley, J. (2001) 'Normalisation, emancipatory research and inclusive research in learning disability'. *Disability and Society.* 16(2): 187–205.

Walmsley, J. and Johnson, K. (2003) *Inclusive Research with People with Learning Disabilities: Past, Present and Futures.* London: Jessica Kingsley.

Whitehurst, T. (2006) 'Liberating silent voices: perspectives of children with profound and complex learning needs on inclusion'. *British Journal of Learning Disabilities.* 35: 55–6.

Wyre Forest Self Advocacy and Tarleton, B. (2005) 'Writing it ourselves'. *British Journal of Learning Disabilities.* 33: 65–69.

Zarb, G. (1992) 'On the road to Damascus: first steps towards changing the social relations to research production'. *Disability, Handicap and Society.* 7: 125–138.

Chapter 9

Making meanings

A talk-based inquiry into adolescent understandings of mental illness

Emma Lindley

This chapter reports its author's experiences of working with a group of Year 10 pupils in a process of inquiry into their understandings and beliefs in relation to mental illness. It describes the use of a photo-vignette discussion technique, demonstrating the ways in which this particular process of inquiry helped to shed light on the ways in which young people make meaning around what is a complex and sensitive theme. The account reveals disturbing findings that could be used to challenge adult perceptions and provoke a debate about implications for school policy and practice. It also illustrates the beneficial impact of working in a small group and demonstrates how humour fed helpfully into the process.

Two key aims guided the inquiry reported in this chapter: the first was my interest in finding out more about how adolescents construct or arrive at understandings of mental illness; and the second was to use this understanding to consider the development of educational processes which may help to reduce discrimination against people with experience of mental health difficulties.

There has been relatively little research focusing on young people's perceptions of mental illness and studies addressing this matter tend to be survey based (e.g. Corrigan *et al.*, 2006; Department of Health, 2007; Watson, 2005). In my view, these studies are in danger of being reductive or oversimplified. One of the problems of investigating people's attitudes and understandings through closed response questions is that there is a very real danger that individualised and personalised meaning-making cannot be properly captured. This work aimed to facilitate open conversations with a small group of teenagers in which they would be at liberty to talk in their own idiom while engaging in tasks designed to enable them to explore the subject of mental illness.

The first stage of the research process was to engage in a phase of pilot work, trialling a number of different approaches to orientating discussions with teenagers about mental illness. Following this, the main body of field-work took place at a state secondary school. I had previously spent time in this particular school with a theatre-in-education company running a drama workshop exploring mental health issues. As a result of this experience, I had developed a positive relationship with the teacher with responsibility for life skills provision within the school. She was extremely accommodating when I approached her to ask if I could work with a small group of Year 10 pupils to more deeply explore their understandings in relation to mental health and illness. Through her, a mixed group of seven Year 10 pupils (aged 14–15) were selected to engage in the discussions with me.

We worked together over the period of a school term, with six hour-long sessions taking place. At the end of each session I interviewed the participants individually. I also conducted follow-up interviews after the end of the series of sessions and again at the beginning of the spring term of 2009. I then held two further workshops in the summer term of 2009, and again, held individual interviews with each of the participants. While I had planned the content and facilitation style of some of the sessions, the intention was always to adopt a fairly fluid style, and to analyse the substance of each discussion in order to develop the content for the next.

Tools for talking

The aim of the group discussion sessions was to encourage conversation and exploration of understandings relating to mental illness. I developed a number of 'springboard' techniques from which to launch conversations, which included a narrative building game, structured reflection on elements of psychiatric diagnosis and discussion of biographical narratives. It is beyond the scope of this chapter to describe all of these in detail but I will present a worked example of one of them – the photo-vignette technique – and demonstrate the ways in which young people engaged with it as a means of inquiry.

I devised a technique for opening conversations about the experience of mental illness without being confined by restrictive or value-laden language which I have called 'photo-vignettes'. The photo-vignette evolved from the starting point of a hunch that using images could be a helpful vehicle for discussion. Initially, I compiled a selection of images of people from *Google Images* searches using terms such as 'mad', 'crazy', 'lunatic', 'depressed', 'druggy', 'alcoholic', 'weird'. I presented a slide show of around 40 images to groups of young people, and asked them to say whatever came into their heads as they looked at each picture. Responses to these images included the following one word replies: 'scared', 'sad', 'lonely', 'weird', 'wrong', 'drunk', 'laughing', 'crying', 'mad'. Notably, there were some similarities between these responses and the search terms I had used, which suggests that the images were communicating extreme emotional or mental states as intended. However, I wanted to find a way of using images to enable more detailed discussion revealing the ways in which young people construct their understandings of mental illness, so I decided upon the addition of a small narrative vignette to each photograph.

The idea was to present young people with a photograph of a fictional character experiencing or exhibiting the types of feelings and behaviours that might indicate that the character has a mental health difficulty – together with a short vignette which provided some information about the fictional character's life. The photograph itself was an important feature in that it gave the sense of a 'real' person being at the heart of the narrative, making it easier for young people to actively engage with the vignette character and to feel empathy with the individuals represented. Figure 9.1 illustrates an example of one of the photo-vignettes used in the discussions.

Each of the young people in the discussion group was given a copy of the photo-vignette to look at, and I read the description underneath the photograph aloud. In this instance, I began the discussion by asking the group to comment on what might be going on for Sarah. The discussions amongst the group about Sarah centred on three key thematic areas. These were:

Figure 9.1 'This is Sarah. She's in your bunch of mates. She's always been quite quiet. Recently she's started getting angry at random times for no apparent reason and saying pretty nasty things to you and your friends, totally unprovoked. You found her in the toilets crying the other day and you've noticed she looks really tired and pale a lot of the time.'

considerations to do with causes and explanations for Sarah's situation; features of 'stress'; and reflections on the social implications of Sarah's behaviour.

The participants all offered explanations rooted in the social world for the behaviour described in the vignette, agreeing that there must be a tangible reason for the changes in her actions. Possible explanations put forward by the participants included domestic violence, divorce, illness in the family and problems with siblings. The belief that there was a reason for Sarah's behaviour seemed to be a factor which resulted in participants feeling generally positive and supportive towards her. One member of the group articulated a feeling that it was both understandable and acceptable to be unusually moody or snappy if it is known that a person is under stress.

When asked how they might respond to Sarah if she were their friend, much seemed to depend on whether or not Sarah disclosed the nature of her problems. One contributor felt that it would simply not be possible to continue a friendship if Sarah's unpredictability and angry outbursts continued indefinitely with no explanation. The prevailing view in this respect was that, if she had been a good friend prior to the changes in behaviour, most would stand by her and be patient. Participants also expressed the view that the angry outbursts were a deliberate plea for help, showing a desire to be noticed. Molly said, 'If you really, really wanted to hide it completely you wouldn't take it out on others, 'cos people are going to start asking.'

This photo-vignette was not intended to depict a set of symptoms denoting a particular specified mental illness diagnosis, but rather to present the types of changes in behaviour which could appear as a result of a range of mental illness experiences. Most of the participants did not approach the character of Sarah with diagnostic labels, with the exception of Simone, who put forward the suggestion that Sarah could have an eating disorder, because of the fact that the vignette mentions she is pale and tired. All of the participants seemed to share the view that Sarah's behaviour was 'ordinary' in that their primary explanation was that she was reacting to challenging life events with understandable changes in mood. This was in spite of the fact that there was no information in the vignette itself about the existence or otherwise of difficult life events. The photo-vignette elicited a narrative response in which the participants built on the information provided to create a more detailed story. This indicated that some degree of empathic ownership of the character was taking place. Members of the group did not express the feeling that Sarah's behaviour was a reason to avoid or shun her. The tone of the conversation very much indicated that the actions of the character in the vignette were within the realm of experience of most of the participants in the discussions – all had a frame of reference through which they were able to identify with Sarah's experience, as described in the photo-vignette.

This photo-vignette worked effectively as a vehicle for stimulating conversation within the realm of mental illness discourse, without framing it explicitly as such. Several other photo-vignettes were also used and these presented characters with more extreme or unsettling behaviours which might appear in serious cases of mental illness. These are presented and discussed in more detail in Lindley (2009). The photo-vignette as a tool of inquiry proved to be very useful within the series of small group discussions held.

Humour and informality

From the outset I was keen that the young people in the discussion group felt able to talk in their own usual language and that the tone of the sessions should be relaxed and informal. One of the ways in which this casual quality was established and sustained was through the allowing of what might have been regarded as tangential or irrelevant humour. Here is an example of the way in which a 'silly' joke became a useful tool for the young people while at the same time triggering their memory of the discussion.

In the first group discussion, I split the group into two smaller groups. Each group was given a large piece of paper and a selection of pens. I asked them to write the words 'mental illness' in the middle of the piece of paper and then to write down anything and everything that came into their minds. I encouraged the group members to talk to each other and to say anything that came to mind. The kinds of words some young people came up with included derogatory or insulting terms that might apply to someone with a mental health problem – for example, 'nutcase', 'bonkers', 'fruitloop'.

During this discussion, one member of the group, Malik, said, 'Pegleg', and wrote this in red capital letters on the piece of paper. All four of the boys in the group found this really funny, laughing and saying, 'Pegleg! Yo pegleg!' to each other. They found this funny because 'pegleg' is a pejorative term applying to a physical disability rather than relating specifically to mental illness. In a way it was just a moment of silliness. However, I let the boys enjoy the moment of humour and did not tell them off for getting off-topic. 'Pegleg' became a sort of motif which ran throughout the rest of the discussion sessions, and the word would be used here and there in later sessions, with the group members laughing about it.

In the final one-on-one interviews, I asked each of the participants to tell me about a particularly memorable moment from the series of discussions we had had. Farzan said:

> Ahhh . . . pegleg, Miss. That was so funny. It was stupid but it was funny. Thing is, whenever I think about pegleg, I think about all that stuff we were talking about – the insults people say about people with mental illness.

I asked him to tell me more about the insults people use, and we then had a rich discussion about acceptable and unacceptable use of language relating to mental illness. For Farzan, the 'pegleg' joke stuck in his mind because it was funny, but he also used the comedy motif as a hook on which to hang some understanding of the more serious content of the work we had done together. Allowing the pegleg conversation to ride out meant that the group members remembered the content of the discussion that had happened around the same time as the joke itself.

The impact of small group inquiry: individual reflections

In this part I present some of the reflections made by individual members of the group during individual conversations with me. Some of these conversations took place at the end of a group discussion session. As I mentioned, I also interviewed each of the participants individually six months after the end of the process.

One of the distinctive features of this process of inquiry was that a small group of young people were taken out of the whole class situation. The atmosphere and tone of the discussion groups was distinctly different from the typical lesson format within school. As a researcher and facilitator, I did not have the same sorts of curricular pressures and restrictions on me that teachers have to negotiate. Consequently, I was able to allow the content of each group session to flow quite organically rather than being tightly defined by the need to meet learning objectives or outcomes. This meant that the way in which the individuals within the group interacted and responded to one another was substantially different to the ways in which they are used to communicating within conventional class structures.

For some members of the group, this method of working made it possible to engage in significant critical discussion; whereas under 'normal' school circumstances they would probably either not participate or make throw-away, silly or displacing comments.

One of the male members, Rahim, talked about this quality of the group in an individual conversation with me at the end of the second group session and told me how surprising this was for him:

> It's pretty interesting to see Farzan and Malik actually taking it seriously. Usually they'd just mess about and say stuff to make us laugh and that. They wouldn't talk about this kind of stuff like this normally.

His comments suggest that the young people in the group were feeling safe enough with the group dynamic to become seriously reflective, and I was pleased that Rahim observed this. It is striking how the response demonstrates not only Rahim's own maturity in being able to reflect, but also how he is able to recognise the capacity of his peers to consider and contemplate the issues.

Molly described a similar feeling during an individual conversation after the fifth meeting of the group:

> The thing about working with you and just the seven of us is that we can say things we wouldn't say in front of the whole class. It's like, I dunno, just really different and when you're talking about mental health stuff, it's loads better to do it like this. In our whole class, people would be a lot sillier and people like me and Rachel just wouldn't dare say anything in case people took the mickey out of us [made fun].

Throughout the group discussion sessions, Molly had always contributed confidently, and was not afraid of disagreeing with her peers or expressing alternative views. Given that this was my experience of her, it was quite surprising to hear her say that she might not dare offer her view in front of the whole class. However, as she herself remarks, it was possibly precisely because of the different ambience of our small group that she had this kind of confidence which enabled her to take risks and contribute freely.

Follow up

Six months later I carried out individual interviews with each of the group members. In these discussions I was interested to find out more about how the process of engagement had impacted on the young people who participated in it after some time had passed.

To stimulate discussion, I selected ten phrases or sentences which the young people had said during the course of the discussion sessions. I put these on cards, and in individual interviews asked the young people to read them through and choose one which stood out for them as having significance or importance to them. In this way I was able to encourage them to reflect on their understanding or interpretation of particular moments during the discussion sessions.

One of the cards read: 'We wouldn't normally talk about this kind of stuff. We'd just avoid it. It would never come up in our conversations.' Rachel selected this card, feeling it was the most meaningful and significant of the selection. She explained that this was particularly important to her because it demonstrated how 'mental illness is something that's very hushed up and it's important that people aren't so frightened of talking about it'. She felt that through engaging in the small group discussions that she was in a better position than her friends who had not taken part in the group:

> My friends understand a lot less than me and don't really know how to speak about this stuff. But I've talked to them about it all, so by doing this with you, I've been able to get them thinking about it when otherwise they wouldn't have.

Rachel's comment also illustrates the way in which she had instigated conversations with others and in doing so was enacting her described need for people to be less afraid of talking about mental illness. The discussion sessions led to her having conversations with peers outside the group about her own developing understanding and thinking about mental illness experience.

Simone chose a card which read 'She's had a bit of a disturbing time or something like that. She's been through a lot. She just sits by herself and cries all the time.' She explained that she couldn't actually remember which bit of our discussion this related to, but that it made her think of a current situation with her neighbour, who has become depressed. Simone said:

> The work we did with you has helped me to understand more about mental illness, and about how people can still be normal with it and need to be treated as themselves by people around them. So, my neighbour, who is depressed, I know that communicating well with her, and just dropping round to spend time with her is really important to boost her confidence. Otherwise she might be like that – just sitting by herself.

Simone implies that the discussion sessions helped her to develop empathy and understanding which she is now able to apply practically to a real world scenario in helping to support a neighbour experiencing depression. It is not possible to say whether Simone might have been the sort of person who would have done this irrespective of having taken part in the sessions with me, but what she says suggests that they were a positive influencing factor.

Asked what stood out as being the most important message to take away from the discussion sessions, Farzan said, 'More or less that mental illness is like . . . well, the people that have them . . . they are just people, you know, with their own story which we need to understand'. He went on to say, 'I know I'll remember it, I know that'. This demonstrates that the impact of participating in the discussions for Farzan was to heighten his feelings of empathy and supportiveness towards people who experience mental health difficulties.

These examples each illustrate distinct positive ways in which the process of inquiry and discussion about issues relating to mental illness impacted upon the young people who took part. Key features which made this approach effective included the use of photo-vignettes which worked to personalise and specify particular mental illness experiences, allowing young people to identify and empathise with the characters presented. The informal tone and flexible form of the discussions which took place was another crucial component which contributed to the success of the approach.

A final thought

This small-scale study demonstrates the way in which carefully orchestrated group discussions can throw light on the attitudes of young people towards a vitally important and yet often overlooked challenge that exists in all schools. The evidence I have presented is powerful and would be valuable in getting staff within a school to discuss current policies and practices and how these might be improved. Clearly, such a discussion would also need very careful management, not least because the themes are potentially troubling.

References

Corrigan, P., Demming Lurie, B., Goldman, H. H., Slopen, N., Medasani, K. and Phelan, S. (2006). 'How adolescents perceive the stigma of mental illness and alcohol abuse'. *Psychiatric Services*, 56: 544–50.

Department of Health (2007). *Attitudes to Mental Illness*. London: Department of Health.

Lindley, E. (2009). 'Gateways to mental illness discourse: tools for talking with teenagers'. *The International Journal of Mental Health Promotion*, 11(1): 15–22(8).

Watson, A. C. (2005). 'Adolescent attitudes toward serious mental illness'. *Journal of Nervous and Mental Disease*, 193(11): 769–772.

Part 3

Creating conversations

Creating conversations, through collecting and analysing evidence in student-friendly ways, about the practice of more equitable forms of education is a key part of the process described in this book. As we have seen, efforts to document and disseminate accounts of practice can make a critical contribution to the further development of inquiry-based approaches. This also draws our attention to the ways in which social learning processes within schools can provide opportunities for developing new responses to learner diversity. However, as those involved are exposed to one another's interpretations of the evidence collected, such processes are rarely straightforward. By focusing on 'creating', rather than simply 'having', conversations, we are acknowledging that there is a highly complex process at work.

With this complexity in mind, the three chapters in this third part look more specifically at the nature of the challenges involved in creating the conversations necessary for the development of purposeful forms of collaboration. Felicity Chambers and her colleagues describe in Chapter 10 how they used children's drawings to stimulate discussions about career aspirations among children, teachers and parents. They found that they needed to ask a series of short questions and conduct follow-up focus groups in order to make sense of the drawings and create a more meaningful conversation.

In Chapter 11, Zoe O'Riordan and Malcolm Williams provide a rich and, at times, very personal account of their research partnership. In so doing, they draw attention to the way that the tensions and dilemmas that occurred stimulated their learning and developed their thinking. They also point to the way that the involvement of 'outsiders' in school-based research can raise uncomfortable issues of power and control. Their research diaries illustrate the kinds of conversations they were having with themselves, and with each other, throughout the process.

This theme is picked up in more detail in Chapter 12, where Abha Sandill describes and reflects on the experience of a team of four research students acting as consultants to a primary school as it investigated issues related to the difficulties many boys faced with writing. This required them to find ways of relating to their partners in the school, and one senior member of staff in particular. An interesting by-product of their involvement was the way the diversity of the members of the team brought further perspectives to the efforts of the school to respond to the diversity of its pupils.

Chapter 10

Using drawing to explore children's aspirations in a primary school

Felicity Chambers, Maria Machalepis and Myriam Mojica Martínez

Finding ways of raising aspirations amongst children from disadvantaged backgrounds is a key challenge in many urban schools. This chapter provides an account of investigations of an initiative in which Year 6 students participated in a scheme organised by local universities, with support from employers, focused on enhancing children's self-esteem and stimulating discussion about career aspirations. The inquiry analysed drawings by students that represented their career aspirations. Focus groups were also conducted with a smaller group of students and they proved invaluable in eliciting a rich discussion about the drawings. The Year 6 students demonstrated a considered approach to their future career opportunities, in contrast to Year 5 students who had not yet been exposed to the initiative.

'Fairview' Primary School has a population of over 500 students. Located in an area of a large city which has a long history of immigration, its students originate from 23 countries and speak 16 different languages. The proportion of students who speak English as an additional language is as high as 98 per cent and 29 per cent have special educational needs. The majority are of Libyan, Pakistani or Somali heritage, and most start school with skills well below what is expected from them at their age.

The staff at Fairview come originally from countries as diverse as Colombia, Greece, India, Pakistan and Thailand, echoing the diversity of the student population. This diversity contributes to the vibrant atmosphere in the school. The classrooms are decorated with children's drawings, written work, sculptures and other art work. These inviting displays give a sense of the inclusive ethos of the school. Initial observations of some of the classes revealed that the staff and students alike were interested and eager to listen to each other's views. The teaching staff encourage the children's participation within group and independent learning, which again emphasises the school's inclusive and nurturing nature.

Our own research team was also extremely diverse. Between us, we speak three languages and have had extremely different educational experiences. Felicity is a maths teacher from the UK, who is currently doing doctoral research with Year 6 students identified as having social, emotional and behavioural difficulties; Myriam is a doctoral student with an interest in the inclusion of autistic children in her home country of Mexico; and Maria has an interest in parent perspectives and comes from Cyprus.

Defining our focus

Fairview School is involved in a scheme called Higher Future for You (HFY). Organised by local universities, with support from local employers, it offers primary school students at the end of Year 5 (aged 9–10) and their teachers opportunities to visit a local university and nearby places of work. The objective is to enhance children's self-esteem and increase their career aspirations. The involvement of parents enables them to have discussions with their children about their career aspirations, and make them aware of each other's views.

A recent report on the aspirations and attainment of young people living in deprived communities concluded that 'Young people's aspirations and those of their parents influence their educational attainment and later life outcomes' (Department for Children, Schools and Families, 2008:2). It therefore seems logical to assume that the more information that can be made available to young people, the more their eyes can be opened to a wide range of potential careers.

Members of staff at Fairview were particularly interested in finding out more about their students' career aspirations. Focusing on this agenda, we supported colleagues in Fairview Primary School to explore the perspectives of students, staff and parents. Beginning with student aspirations, we proceeded to explore parents' aspirations for their children, as well as the influence of school staff on students' views.

Following discussions with members of the school leadership team, we decided to explore the aspirations of Year 5 students who had not yet participated in the HFY scheme, and to assess how they differed from students in Year 6 (aged 10–11) who had completed the scheme. The answers to these questions were important for the school, as they were keen for students to think about their future, and to reinforce the key role that education can play in helping them reach their potential. Through this inquiry, staff at Fairview hoped to gain a better understanding of both the students' and parents' aspirations for their children, how these could be developed further, and whether to use more time and resources in encouraging students to consider a wider range of career opportunities.

We began our inquiry by observing a Year 6 class who had participated in the Higher Futures for You scheme and a Year 5 class that was about to embark on the scheme. The purpose of the observations was to immerse ourselves in the day-to-day life of Fairview School, as well as to become familiar with the two groups of children. From these observations, we were able to brainstorm some ideas about possible methods of inquiry for exploring children's aspirations. In this chapter we focus primarily on how our inquiry helped to create a series of conversations about young people's aspirations.

Focusing on aspirations through drawing

We decided to use drawings as a method of inquiry and as a stimulus to encourage conversations with the children about their career aspirations. We had noticed during our observations that some of the students were quite shy and so we decided that asking them to draw, rather than do role plays or answer questions, would put them at ease.

Drawing makes a connection with the imagination and can help children feel confident to express their opinions without feeling intimidated, or thinking that there is a 'right' answer which they must give. Anning and Ring (2004) have argued that visual methods can engage children and young people in a holistic, creative and practical way. Such creative activities can add an important dimension to the narrative process by eliciting insights that would be difficult to capture through talk or writing. More importantly, we chose to use drawing since many students in these two classes struggled with the English language and some had associated learning difficulties.

In planning our approach, we read about the work of others who had carried out similar investigations. So, for example, MacPhail and Kinchin (2004) carried out a study of the experience of 46 students in Year 5 who participated in a school sports programme. During the inquiry they found that 'the drawings completed by students allowed them to express their own observations and experiences of Sport Education without being steered by the teachers' agenda or the researchers' likely bias in conducting interviews and making observations' (MacPhail and Kinchin, 2004:104). However, as we will explain, our experience was different and we struggled to interpret the drawings.

We decided to pilot the use of drawings with a Year 4 class (aged 8–9 years) in order to assess its effectiveness and possible strengths and weaknesses. We introduced the topic of future aspirations to the students, using prompts to help them answer questions, such as, 'Where will you be in 20 years?' and 'What will your job be?' We asked them to work individually and draw their responses to the questions.

Overall, the pilot study suggested that:

- students' ideas were limited to the most common and well-known occupations (i.e. football player, teacher, doctor);

- a number of students focused on their academic achievements, rather than on occupational or future plans for further education;
- students who were sitting together tended to produce drawings on the same theme.

In response to the pilot study findings, we decided to include an introductory warm-up activity in our main inquiry in which every member of the two classes (Year 5 and Year 6) participated. We hoped that the warm-up activity would help students to brainstorm a variety of jobs and occupations, and recall the jobs they knew and might like to pursue when they leave school. Furthermore, in order to avoid students simply copying each other's ideas, we *asked them* to pay close attention to their own drawings rather than looking at others'. We also provided plenty of supervision during the main drawing activity.

When considering the drawings generated in the pilot study, we realised that the analysis would be difficult, as drawings mean different things to different people. For instance, looking at one particular picture, we were unsure of what the student was trying to portray and different team members interpreted the drawings differently.

Introducing writing and focus groups

We decided to add a writing element to the drawing activity in order to overcome the difficulty faced in the pilot inquiry in analysing the children's drawings. Since many students had difficulties in expressing themselves in English, we decided to create short, open-ended questions which would

Figure 10.1 Aspiring to be 'a plane mechanic'. A drawing by a pupil in Year 5.

Figure 10.2 Aspiring to be a lawyer, with back-up choices listed. A drawing by a pupil in Year 6.

enable us to gain a deeper insight into the students' aspirations. We also asked the students to complete a series of unfinished short sentences, allowing them the freedom to write as much or as little as they wanted, for example about their parents' aspirations for them. This allowed the students to add words to the drawings if they were having difficulty representing their ideas in the form of drawings. This writing-based section of the activity gave those students who do not enjoy drawing the opportunity to express their ideas through text, as 'combinations of visual and text-based qualitative approaches are often fruitful and potentially insightful' (Prosser and Loxley, 2007:56). Finally, when everyone had completed the activity, the students were invited to talk about their drawings in front of their class.

We then organised two focus groups – one with six Year 5 students and another with eight Year 6 students. The selection of the two sub-groups was made after an analysis of all the drawings, in combination with the written information. Students were chosen to provide as representative a sample of each class as possible, with a range of drawings from those that were very in-depth and detailed, to those which contained minimal information.

We decided that interviewing each individual child would have been disruptive to the students' lessons, and that focus groups would be beneficial

Figure 10.3 Aspiring to be a doctor and reflections on the journey ahead. A drawing by a pupil in Year 6.

for many reasons. They gave us the opportunity to observe the interaction between, and contrasting opinions of, the children. In this way, we brought together 'a specifically chosen sector of the population to discuss a particular given theme or topic' (Cohen *et al.*, 2007:376). Moreover, this gave us an additional opportunity to make more sense of the drawings.

The students had an opportunity to talk more about what they had drawn, and this gave us a chance to gain a greater understanding of the drawings. In the majority of cases, the overall theme of the job aspiration was clear (for example, a picture of a singer or footballer), but the details regarding the location of the job, why the students wanted this career, or how they had arrived at this aspirational point in the future was not at all clear in the picture. However, these pictures were a great way to start a conversation within the focus group. The students were not 'cold' to the questions posed to them, they had already thought about their aspirations and had some ideas even if they were fairly simple.

The focus group with the Year 5 students only lasted about 10 minutes, since the students were just answering our questions in one-word sentences. This made us realise that the children had not thought a great deal about their aspirations, and that this was the first time that they had been asked to

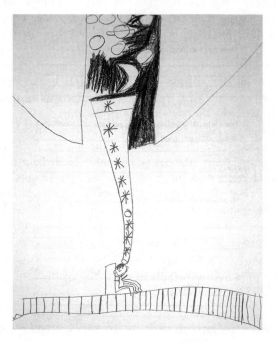

Figure 10.4 Aspiring to be an astronomer. A drawing by a pupil in Year 6.

consider their future. It also transpired that they did not know precisely what their parents wanted them to be, as they had not discussed this issue with them. Celebrity jobs, such as football player, singer or fashion model, were more popular in the Year 5 group. Most of the pupils mentioned the money they would earn from a job as their main criterion for selecting a career.

The focus group with the Year 6 students led to a richer form of data. This group was much more talkative. They were also far more actively involved with the task of thinking about their future. All of them were in a position to analyse their thinking regarding their decisions by giving explanations as to how they had arrived at their future plans. For instance, they mentioned relatives or family friends who seemed to be role models for the careers they had chosen. All of them had back-up plans – in some cases even more than one – and they were able to explain the necessity of having back-up plans. Significantly, all the participants in this group had considered, and wanted to pursue, advanced studies at a university as a means of securing what they perceived to be a good job. When the Year 6 students were asked what they believed their parents would like them to become, they mentioned jobs that were mostly similar to their own preferences. However, they did not seem to have been influenced by their parents' choices.

Neither the Year 5 students nor those in Year 6 had had many discussions with their parents regarding their aspirations and future plans. Those who had discussed their plans with parents reported that these conversations were mostly with their mothers, since many of their fathers worked outside the UK. All the participants gave examples of discussions they had had with their teachers about their plans, implying that the teachers potentially had greater influence over their aspirations. This point was verified by the Year 6 teacher when we held a focus group with the staff.

The influence of the Higher Futures for You project on the Year 6 students was clearly considerable. They had found the project both interesting and useful, and explained how the activities had helped them to develop their ideas and consider the possibility of studying at a university. The project had raised their awareness of the availability of different kinds of jobs and careers, and the opportunities associated with them. They had also been encouraged to develop a more realistic approach to choosing a career, and the process had helped them to consider their future more seriously. The aspirations emerging both from the Year 6 drawings and subsequent focus groups were related to achievable and realistic jobs – unlike the Year 5 students who had selected many unrealistic options.

Reflecting on the collaborative inquiry experience

The drawing activity was successful in engaging the majority of children in the inquiry. The freedom to be creative, and add words or sentences to their drawings as their thinking developed, was a real benefit to the approach we adopted. A small minority claimed that they were 'no good at drawing', and were hesitant about participating. However, by the end of the activity, even these children became engaged. The main problem arose from the difficulty in interpreting the drawings. The open-ended sentences and focus groups were essential in providing further insight into their meaning. The focus groups provided additional inspiration for many students who were able to add details to their aspirations as a result of listening to other people's ideas. This would not have been possible in an interview situation.

The most striking finding was the differences between the two age groups in their drawings and the quality of the focus group discussions. The Year 6 students seemed to be more prepared than the Year 5 students to make decisions about the future and to explain the procedure that led them to make these decisions. Additionally, the Year 6 students had considered their future more seriously and were aware of a variety of different occupations, indicating that they had been influenced by the HFY initiative.

Conducting research with children presents a major challenge in terms of identifying alternative and innovative research methods with which to explore their views in as genuine a way as possible. This inquiry gave us the opportunity to develop a series of creative research methods. Drawings were a method that not only gave us some interesting findings, but that the children really enjoyed. The drawing activity demanded a small amount of time and effort, fitted easily into the children's classroom environment and allowed them to be as creative as they wished.

We learned the benefits of working collaboratively as part of a team: each member of our team brought different, and at times apparently unequal, skills to the inquiry. However, together we had organisational skills, a variety of communication skills and experience, and varying degrees of time management. Only one team member had prior experience of the English school system and although she played a critical role at the beginning, she developed a serious illness part way through the inquiry, leaving the two non-English researchers to play a more central role than would otherwise have been the case.

We have learned, too, that there is no magic recipe for conducting an inquiry in a primary school. It is a process that stretches the researchers' thinking, creativity and ability to respond to ever-changing circumstances. We found that it was essential to be adaptable to fit in with the needs of the school, and with the children's schedules, personalities and varying abilities. We had to be flexible in terms of the research timeline and make changes in accordance with time and resource constraints.

References

Anning, A. and Ring, K. (2004) *Making sense of children's drawings*. Maidenhead: Open University Press.

Cohen, L., Manion, L. and Morrison, K. (2007) *Research methods in education*. (6th edition). London: Routledge.

Department for Children, Schools and Families (DCSF) (2008) *Aspirations and attainment amongst young people in deprived communities: analysis and discussion paper*. London: DCSF and Cabinet Office. Available online at: www.cabinetoffice. gov.uk/media/109339/aspirations_evidence_pack.pdf (accessed 7 January 2010).

MacPhail, A. and Kinchin, G. (2004) The use of drawings as an evaluative tool: students' experiences of sport education. *Physical Education and Sport Pedagogy* 9(1): 87–108.

Prosser, J. and Loxley, A. (2007) Enhancing the contribution of visual methods to inclusive education. *Journal of Research in Special Educational Needs* 7(1): 55–68.

Chapter 11

Researching student voice in a special school

Insider/outsider dilemmas of power, ethics and loyalties

Zoe O'Riordan and Malcolm Williams

This chapter describes a project that set out to explore ways in which students might contribute to a school's staff selection process. A range of methods was trialled to explore the extent to which young people were capable of engaging in such a crucial and sensitive part of school life. In addition, staff members were interviewed about their thoughts on these processes. Power relations are important in any collaborative inquiry. In this context they were particularly challenging. Conflict and dilemmas arose around: ethics and confidentiality; differing professional practices; communication failures and the pressures of other commitments; and divided loyalties. These dilemmas ultimately deepened and energised the research process. The project provided valuable lessons about the management of power in such contexts.

Take two opinionated, driven, passionate practitioners and one research question; add a group of students with social, emotional and behavioural difficulties; stir in a hefty power imbalance, professional conflicts and divided loyalties; combine with busy schedules and limited time, and what do you get? Surprisingly – a successful collaborative inquiry that can play a part in developing more inclusive practices within a special school.

This chapter describes an inquiry conducted by Malcolm, a teacher at the school and part-time student, and Zoe, a full-time student and ex-youth/care worker. The aim of the research was to explore the potential for students to become involved in their school's staff selection process. This was not an easy issue to explore, particularly in a special school for students with social, emotional and behavioural difficulties, even with managerial support.

Power relations are integral to any collaborative inquiry. We had to manage issues of power in relation to students and staff, and between ourselves. Malcolm's insider status offered benefits, such as easy access to student information and straightforward contact with the staff. However, it also created a power imbalance within the research team. Malcolm was the gate-keeper, controlling knowledge, access and movement.

Tensions and dilemmas arose around:

- ethics and confidentiality;
- differing professional practices;
- communication failures and the pressures of other commitments;
- divided loyalties.

On reflection, however, we believe that these same tensions and dilemmas ultimately deepened and energised the inquiry process. At the same time, our individual and collaborative journeys through this project taught us valuable lessons about the management of power.

The rationale

The inquiry was conducted in 'Bank Hall', a local-authority-funded, 55-place special school for students aged 9–16. Although the school is mixed, the vast majority of the students are boys. The school management team was very outwards looking, and keen to engage with processes of research for purposes of moving policy and practice forward. They already had a vibrant and meaningful student council, but wanted to increase their use of the student voice in the development of the school. Through discussion with senior staff, we decided to explore the possibility of involving students in recruitment processes.

Even with the full support of the management team, exploring student involvement in recruitment was contentious. It involves giving children power over the lives of adults, a difficult concept in any school, but in a school for pupils with social, emotional and behavioural difficulties, where adult authority is routinely and aggressively challenged every day, it was verging on dangerous. However, we felt it worth exploring, since, if managed correctly, 'it can empower young people so that they can participate more effectively in the decisions that affect their lives' (Treseder, 1997, p. 70), as required by the *Children Act 1989* (The Stationery Office, 1989) and the *United Nations Convention on the Rights of the Child* (United Nations, 1989).

If the challenge was greater in a special school, then so were the potential rewards. Research into students with social, emotional and behavioural difficulties suggests that they see lack of understanding of their needs, and a failure to build productive relationships with adults, as key contributors to their inability to remain in mainstream schools (Wise, 1999; Gadour, 2006; De Pear, 1995). Indeed, Cooper (1993) and Polat and Farrell (2002) have found that when students with social, emotional and behavioural difficulties attending special schools talk about their schooling they invariably talk about relationships they have built with staff and how these have contributed to their success.

Many schools have taken the idea of pupil voice on board (e.g. developing school councils, consulting with pupils on new school buildings, etc). However, there is little evidence that we have located about young people being allowed to become involved in decisions relating to what is, perhaps, the most important element of their school lives: the adults who work with them.

To explore the issue of pupil involvement in staff selection we broke the task into three parts in order to find out:

- whether the students knew, and were realistic about, what they wanted from their staff;
- whether the students could negotiate a selection criteria, taking into account employment issues, such as equal opportunities;
- what the current staff thought about the idea of student involvement in staff recruitment.

Working with students

We worked with a group of six 13–14-year-old boys. They were selected because they were available, old enough to understand the issues and likely to be able to participate fully in the research process. Data were collected through three activities:

- one-to-one 'informant'-style interviews (Powney and Watts, 1987);
- a group categorisation activity;
- group discussions.

The *one-to-one interviews* were designed to allow the students to speak freely and independently about what they wanted from their staff, without being influenced by each other's opinions. They were given the option of using the body map (see Figure 11.1), mind maps or any other way of expressing and recording their views. The body map we devised was used by most of the participants (four out of six) to think about different aspects of their staff. The students gave their own labels to different parts of the body, and allocated one half to positive characteristics, the other to negative ones. Of the two participants who did not use the body map, one used a mind map, the other simply drew a line down the middle of his page and wrote what he wanted from the staff on one side, and what he did not want on the other.

By giving the students choice in how they expressed their views, we allowed for their varied academic ability, in that no pressure was put on them to read or write. This ensured that we did not cause embarrassment: the activity was supposed to be empowering, not humiliating. The students were able to express their views in their own ways, so the data they produced truly belonged to them, increasing its validity.

We analysed the data collected in one-to-one interviews, drawing from it a range of words that the students had used to describe what they did and did not want from their staff. We then used these in the second activity, a *classification exercise* which allowed students to express their personal preferences and priorities. We gave the students cards with the words written on them, which they then placed in hoops labelled: *Really want it, Want it, Don't want it, Really don't want it*, and *Not bothered*. This gave us an understanding of the students' priorities and acted as a member check, since the 'not bothered' category allowed them to get rid of anything that they did not feel was important.

The *group discussions* were led by the outsider, Zoe, since her experience in youth work meant that she was used to facilitating group work with all kinds of young people. She was able to support the students in a non-directive manner. Through this group process, we extracted a selection of descriptive words from our earlier list which had proved most popular with the students. We wrote these words on a white board and encouraged the groups to discuss them and decide which were most important. They also discussed contentious issues, such as gender, age and 'sportiness', to develop a consensus about their staff selection criteria.

By the end of this activity we could say with some confidence that these students knew, and agreed on, what they wanted from their staff (the words in parentheses are their words). In summary they valued staff who:

Figure 11.1 The body map developed by Zoe.

- *interacted* with them in certain ways (active, plays games);
- had particular *interpersonal skills and attitudes* (friendly, funny, cool, relaxed, calm, helpful);
- were *empathic* (listens, understanding, talks to you, gives space, notices you).

Perhaps more importantly, the students were able to engage with issues such as equal opportunities. They could also understand that whilst they did not all share the same priorities in the characteristics they wanted most from their staff, they needed to have a range of people working with them, with different attributes and skills.

Impact and limitations

All members of staff were invited to participate, and we ensured that those who did were representative of the staff as a whole in terms of age, gender, experience and role. We interviewed members of staff only once. We considered using group interviews, but in the end decided that they were unlikely to want to co-operate if we imposed too heavily on their time. For reasons of convenience they were all interviewed by Malcolm.

The staff made it clear that, in their view, students have no place on a staff selection panel. The main reason cited was the potential for students to exploit their new position of power. This view was unanimous. They did not believe that the students were capable of taking the appointment of staff sufficiently seriously to be given control over the careers of adults. They felt that student involvement should be limited to 'meet and greet' prospective staff, or a similarly narrow and shallow engagement in the recruitment process.

With more time we could have taken the research further but we had to be practical about what we could achieve. We feel we may not have made enough allowances for the fact that we were working with students with social, emotional and behavioural difficulties. On occasion, some students did not fully engage with the activities. Whilst the insider position allowed us to keep our finger on the pulse, and identify when individual pupils were struggling, it is possible that we relied too much on the insider's position, relationships and influence within the school.

However, we were able to demonstrate to the senior leadership team that, with appropriate intervention and support, these students could engage in a debate about what they needed from their staff, accommodating different perspectives and considering issues such as equal opportunities. We felt that if only the staff could have seen the constructive way in which the young people engaged with the debate, their views on the potential for pupil involvement in recruitment could have been challenged.

We had limited contact with the staff (partly in recognition of Malcolm's position in the school) and this may have reduced the potential impact of the research through our failure to engage them more deeply in the process. But we gave the school a starting point. Those in the school are now aware of the gap which exists between the students' capacity to be involved in recruitment procedures, and staff belief in them. Malcolm is continuing to work with the school on bridging this gap.

Our development as researchers

Most research reports end at this point. The research has been described and justified in a way that is honest and transparent, and so can be judged. The inquiry was in many ways a success: aims were met and questions answered. However, some of the most important lessons we learnt tend not to be addressed in a traditional research report. The research protocols we followed, drawn from the study of research methods and ethical guidelines, failed to provide guidance on some of the most challenging aspects of the research.

Frustrations set in at different times throughout the process, which could have derailed the whole project. The research brought up interesting questions about us, not just as researchers but also as professional practitioners and people with different histories and experiences. We realised that it was not just about 'us' looking at 'them', but also about 'us' looking at 'us'. And in both contexts, doing this through critical and reflective eyes.

We were encouraged to keep reflective diaries, to include such things as worries, emotions, ideas and progress. Borg (2001) has discussed at length the benefits of keeping a research journal. Similar to him, we each initially wondered as to the benefit of the research journal. We have since acknowledged the power of such a journal in developing our understanding and helping us to understand everyone involved in this research, including ourselves and each other. In reviewing the research and our roles in it, our diaries have been invaluable.

Here is the story, not told by the research report, but held in our diaries.

The beginning

Malcolm: Collaborative inquiry does not just happen; it has to be worked at. This includes compromises, adopting new approaches and being open to criticism. I was researching familiar ground; my school. I had my project planned, but then I was given a research colleague that I did not wish for.

This was now 'our' research project, not mine. This created a personal conflict because I had already mapped out the research process I was going to undertake. I had an agenda, I had no one else to consider. Was this selfish? Probably! My aim was to get in, get on with it and then get out and move on. I was considering a straight path with no deviations. I set the path and I wanted to walk it alone.

My initial contact with Zoe was professional and civil. It was now official, my research was now a team collaborative inquiry. My first diary entry reads: 'Discussion with Zoe regarding working with me – no problems' (1 October 2007).

I guess I was just being polite. How could I possibly know that there would be no problems? Here, suddenly I was required to be part of a team. Most of my working life has been in teams, but this team was being imposed upon me. Suddenly I had to be flexible, accommodating and open to new approaches. I can be all of those things above when the conditions are right and working in my favour, but now I was going out of my comfort zone!

Zoe was happy to continue with my research idea. Her approach was proving to be surprisingly refreshing in that I could now see the research from a different point of view and this allowed me to be not just reflective but also critical.

Zoe: From the start I knew that Malcolm had planned to conduct this research project alone. He knew what he was going to look at, and roughly how he planned to do it. He was going to work in his own school, to his own timeframe: alone. Then I joined him. I was aware that he might resent my presence, which was bound to make the research process more logistically difficult.

Added to this, it soon became apparent that our different professional backgrounds gave us different approaches to working with children. As a youth worker, I was used to working in a non-directive manner, facilitating discussions, not leading them. As a teacher (particularly of students with social, emotional and behavioural difficulties), Malcolm was used to directing the students and maintaining fairly tight control at all times. Furthermore, his power within the research process was absolute. Most doors in the school were locked, and he had the keys. He held information about the students that I had no access to. All my interactions with school staff were mediated through his existing relationships with them.

Dealing with the tensions that my status as a powerless outsider gave rise to was the most challenging aspect of the research, but I began the project positively, seeing some of the potential pitfalls, but as yet unaware of how significant they would be: 'The insider/outsider dynamic shows great potential, but will continue to rest on Malcolm's willingness to consider the suggestions I naively come up with, and me being able to have my "bright ideas" curbed . . . Malcolm has control of my movement and contact with pupils, but our relationship is that of peers, so I can challenge him.' (early October 2007).

The middle

Fuelled by our optimism, we embarked on planning our research. However, as time passed, the degree of challenge that collaboration presented became apparent in ways we had not foreseen. In the planning stage our concerns were with our power over the students, and Malcolm's relationship with the staff. But it became apparent that the power relation that needed the most attention was between ourselves.

Malcolm: We both have our own unique strengths and we did work to these strengths. However, we must not forget that I was researching the familiar; I was the insider, Zoe was the outsider. Indeed, I wrote in my diary: 'I feel that this project may be useful, however, I fear that my relationship with the school may cloud my judgements. I must ensure that Zoe knows of my fears and concerns' (11 October 2007).

This was a clear indication that I was now considering Zoe as my research colleague. My concerns were to do with issues of ethics and loyalty. These became a constant humming in my head. I had loads of school information but I was just not prepared to share any of it except that which was absolutely necessary. This was a rigid approach. I even on occasions dismissed Zoe's ideas and suggestions without explanation. I had power over my colleague. I wrote in my diary: 'What harm would it do to pass on the information?' (late October 2007).

We were colleagues but our relationship was unequal. I did discuss this issue on occasions to show I was aware of this awkward situation.

Zoe: The imbalance of power between us did create problems. Balancing our commitments beyond the research meant that it was often squeezed into far too small a space in our lives. This led to occasional breakdowns in communication as we each dealt with more pressing matters. For me, this emphasised my outsider status and lack of power within the research process, but honest discussion of problems when they arose, together with sensitivity towards each other's position within the research, enabled us to maintain positive relationships: 'Was cross with Malcolm for not communicating – perhaps nose is out of joint because of feeling of powerlessness. Glad we could sort it out quickly. Think we're both fairly open/ transparent people: makes it easier' (early November, 2007).

I tried to use my increased sensitivity over issues of power constructively within the research, to improve my engagement with the students and increase my reflexivity: 'Awareness of inequality of power relations between me and Malcolm possibly made me more sensitive towards participants. Avoided being directive, very conscious of soft, supportive hand, not shove in right direction! . . . It was difficult having to negotiate my place in the project: being reliant on Malcolm. But his approach made me comfortable – giving me control, checking back, etc.' (late November 2007).

But at times I made unfair judgements about my co-researcher: 'Malcolm seems inclined to direct. Think it helps not to be a teacher, relate to young people in a completely different way' (November 2007). This may have been, in part, a way of boosting my own feeling of value within the research: that even though I felt I had so little control I was an essential part of it.

The end

By the time we finished the project we had learnt vital lessons: about the value of working as a team; of seeing life from each other's personal and professional viewpoints; and of challenging ourselves to think critically about assumptions we make and things we do.

Malcolm: Could I have handled the situation differently? Possibly. I suppose it would have been easy to discuss my dilemma with senior school staff and a compromise could have been brokered which would have opened doors for Zoe to help her answer her own questions. However, I did not pursue this initiative. I held the power and to this day I do not really know why I made it difficult for myself, except to say that if I opened the floodgates slightly then I just do not know if I would have passed on sensitive information, even innocently. This ethical dilemma needs to be considered prior to data collection. This and other ground rules in relation to such things as loyalties should be discussed to ensure that neither researcher is placed in a difficult situation.

My loyalty to the students had an impact on my approach as a researcher. It was not just their privacy I had to guard, but our ongoing relationship. I could not act differently when in research mode. They knew me, I knew them: we had created boundaries. This was a negative aspect of being an insider; established relationships and rules of conduct had been set: they could not be changed just for this project.

Zoe: Whilst Malcolm continued to struggle with questions that are, perhaps, unanswerable, relating to loyalties, professional judgements and all the complexities involved in researching your own workplace, my conclusions were somehow easier. I had less power within the research, but I was also less intensively involved, with both the project and the school. I would not have any responsibility for taking the ideas we had explored further, and could walk away.

My experience in this project has sharpened my understanding of the way my participants feel within the research process. But more than that, I learnt to work with, rather than against, the power of others. Where necessary, I use their influence or authority to help me gain access to people or information, negotiating my way in. I also find that I can use my own lack of power in research situations to encourage people to talk openly to me, since they need not feel threatened by me. Malcolm gave me insights into the position of the practitioner who engages with a researcher which I could not have gained in any other way.

Finally, I learnt to be more reflective, viewing my own practice through the same critical lens as I had viewed others. For example: 'Working with someone else has made me look at myself and my way of working in a way that working alone couldn't. Malcolm has a very different approach, and initially I thought him too directive with the children, but now I see we've worked in a complementary way, and I need to be more directive at times to get the job done' (December 2007).

Making sense of our collaboration

Our joint conclusion is that the most important lesson from this collaboration is that applied research of this sort must start with understanding the needs and concerns of those involved. In this sense it is, initially at least, less about the topic or methods and much more the researchers' roles, histories, personalities and professional backgrounds. It is worth noting here that BERA (2004) presents relevant guidance in relation to three areas of responsibility: in relation to participants, sponsors of research and to the community of educational researchers. In so doing, it offers suggestions regarding the working conditions of research staff, but it gives nothing in relation to conflicts of interest and power between co-researchers. This, we feel, is worthy of further exploration and clarification.

We embarked on this project as keen, well-intentioned practitioner-researchers. We feel that we completed it as more enlightened individuals, with developed empathic qualities. We both agree that power is a commodity which, if understood in the beginning, can be used constructively in research processes. Questions of power, sensitively managed in the context of both the researchers and the inquiry process, may well be the key to the success of the project. And were we to start this collaborative inquiry again, it is with these issues that we would begin.

References

BERA (2004) *Revised Ethical Guidelines for Ethical Research*, Slough: British Educational Research Association.

Borg, S. (2001) The research journal: a tool for promoting and understanding researcher development. *Language Teaching Research*, 5: 156–177.

Cooper, P. (1993) Learning from pupils' perspectives. *British Journal of Special Education*, 20: 129–133.

De Pear, S. (1995) Perceptions of pupils with special needs. In M. Lloyd-Smith and J. Dwyfor-Davies, (eds) *On the Margins: The Educational Experiences of 'Problem' Pupils*, Stoke-on-Trent, Trentham Books.

Gadour, A. (2006) Libyan children's views on the importance of school factors which contributed to their emotional and behavioural difficulties. *School Psychology International*, 27(2): 171–191.

Polat, F. and Farrell, P. (2002) What was it like for you? Former pupils' reflections on their placement at a residential school for pupils with emotional and behavioural difficulties. *Emotional and Behavioural Difficulties*, 7: 97–108.

Powney, J. and Watts, M. (1987) *Interviewing in Educational Research*, London, Routledge.

The Stationery Office (1989) *Children's Act 1989*, London, The Stationery Office.

Treseder, P. (1997) *Empowering Young People*, London, Save the Children.

United Nations (1989) *United Nations Convention on the Rights of the Child*, New York, United Nations.

Wise, S. F. (1999) Improving success in the mainstream for pupils with emotional and behavioural difficulties. *Pastoral Care in Education*, 17(3): 14–20.

Chapter 12

Collaborative inquiry

What's in it for schools?

Abha Sandill

This chapter provides an account of a collaborative inquiry carried out in an urban primary school that focused on boys' underachievement. This theme emerged through discussions involving staff and four university students who acted as co-researchers to the school. Research methods used included: picture-elicitation with individual children, staff questionnaires, classroom observations, focus group discussions with children and staff interviews. There was an emerging focus on the importance of student voice as the inquiry progressed. A key feature of the account is the way it throws light on the social complexity involved when 'outsiders' work alongside school staff in using an inquiry-based approach.

My account is of a study I carried out with three other members of the M.Ed programme at the University of Manchester. Our task was to work with colleagues in the school in carrying out research that could contribute to the school's efforts to respond to learner diversity. This meant that it was vital that we developed good working relationships with key staff in the school.

We were keen to carry out an inquiry that would have an impact on school policy and practice. Our lectures and reading had provided a basic framework for a collaborative research process but it was still up to us to develop our own unique approach. Although all four group members had previous experience of engaging in collaborative work as part of previous studies and teaching responsibilities, only one student (myself) had participated in a collaborative research inquiry – and my experience had been in India.

In this chapter, I share with you how the process of inquiry unfolded in partnership with the school. In doing so, I highlight challenges that arose during the research process in working collaboratively as a group of students from diverse cultural and educational backgrounds in the Netherlands, Greece, India and the UK. This group diversity added to the complexity of conducting a collaborative inquiry but it also brought new interpretations to the English context.

I also reflect on the way we, as visitors to the school, managed some of the challenges involved and the ways in which colleagues in the school assisted us in overcoming them. This leads me to identify factors that facilitated the collaborative research process and led to positive outcomes for the student researchers and, indeed, for the school staff and their pupils.

Setting the agenda

St Anthony's is a Catholic school serving an area of multiple deprivation in the north of England. The community in which the school is located was, until recently, relatively homogenous. However, increasing numbers of pupils from minority ethnic communities now attend the school. While striving to maintain a strong ethos based on Catholic principles and a caring environment for all of its pupils, the school also aims to achieve high standards in their personal, academic and social development.

The school was approached by the university because of its commitment to developing an inclusive ethos through its participation in *The Manchester Inclusion Standard* (MIS), a review instrument developed by the local authority, in collaboration with a research team from the University of Manchester (Moore *et al.*, 2007). The school's development plan regularly incorporated progress on MIS indicators and this was reviewed periodically.

During the initial phase of the inquiry, we had a joint meeting with Mr Martin, the head teacher, and the inclusion coordinator, Mrs Harris, to identify the topic of research. Based on their latest review of MIS progress, Mrs Harris highlighted two issues that were of great concern to the school: underachievement of Key Stage 2 students (aged 7–11) in science, and of boys in all year groups in literacy, particularly in writing.

After discussion, we took a collaborative decision to research underachievement of boys in literacy, as it was a whole school issue. Moreover, it seemed possible that achievement in language might be affecting the levels of attainment in science.

The involvement of two key members of staff, the head teacher and the inclusion coordinator, right from the beginning of the project served two key purposes: it established the importance of the research task for the school and also validated our role as researchers for other staff members. During the course of the inquiry, Mrs Harris became an integral member of our research team. As the inclusion coordinator and a member of the senior management team, her keen involvement proved very fruitful to the success of the project. Essentially, her cooperative efforts opened up our access to both material and human resources within the school. The school's overall commitment to the research process influenced our commitment and enthusiasm for the inquiry as it progressed.

Valuing a diverse team

Both Mr Martin and Mrs Harris were intrigued by the diversity that our team brought to the task. Not only did we represent different nationalities, but our educational backgrounds and experience of working with schools varied enormously. Irene was an exchange student from the Netherlands who was keen to become familiar with English schools – she was the youngest member of our team. Anna was a psychology graduate and experienced primary school teacher from Greece. Zoa was the only team member who was born and brought up in England – a qualified teacher of Pakistani heritage, Zoa added to the diversity of our team. Finally, I am a trained teacher and researcher from India, currently studying for a doctorate. I was familiar with the education system in India, where I had worked on a national-level research project to explore inclusive school settings and briefly lectured in child development.

Such diversity could have been viewed with concern, but our partners in the school saw this as an advantage. Specifically, they seemed to see it as providing a learning opportunity and were eager to know what we thought about the issue of boys' underachievement. They asked us, for example, is this also an issue in India or Greece?

Beyond our different backgrounds, we each brought different strengths to the table. Each member took the initiative to perform tasks for which they possessed the relevant skills. We had an informal group leader who coordinated the inquiry, and whom we all trusted and supported in all possible ways. Although we had a 'leader', each member felt responsible for their own individual task and for the success of the inquiry as a whole. This was particularly evident during the later stages of research, for example, at the time of collating all the information collected, analysing the data, making presentations and writing up the final report. This sort of understanding between the team members developed over time, as we engaged in a cyclical process of action and reflection (Bray *et al.*, 2000) to examine the research issue at hand. I return to the details of our team's collaborative efforts later in the chapter.

Pursuing a broader notion of inclusion

Three of our team members came from settings where inclusion as a concept was still in its infancy and only had rhetorical significance. For us, previously, inclusion was largely associated with the education of children with disabilities. Indeed, St Anthony's School had some children with disabilities on roll who were studying in regular classes. Structural and curricular changes had been made over the years to accommodate the needs of these children and, as far as we could see, there were no issues of immediate concern regarding their education.

For our colleagues in the school, boys' underachievement was of far greater concern. This focus helped us understand the broader concept and definition of inclusive education, as it operates in the English policy context, where the concern is with a much wider range of learners vulnerable to marginalisation, exclusion and underachievement (Ainscow *et al.*, 2006). During lectures we had learned that increasingly within international policy debates inclusion is seen as being about finding ways of responding to 'all' children, irrespective of race, ethnicity, class, gender or ability (e.g. UNESCO, 1994) and that locally, within the *Inclusion Standard*, this involved ensuring the presence, participation and achievement of all children. However, our experiences in our home countries told us a different story, and initially we were confused. This was in itself a valuable learning experience.

Engaging with a theoretical understanding of boys' underachievement in writing shed light on broader educational issues and day-to-day issues in English schools and so brought the university lectures alive. The literature revealed the importance of addressing the underachievement of boys, and of attending to race and gender issues, in order to improve educational outcomes and develop more informed policies (Jones and Myhill, 2004a, 2004b; Smith, 2003).

Researching the issue

Once the research agenda was set, we narrowed our focus and methodology to tie in closely with the issue of underachievement among boys in literacy and writing. Our prime research question was, *Why do boys underachieve in writing?*

Our overall purpose was to explore the nature of challenges that pupils seemed to be facing in their literacy classes and review practices in the school that supported literacy and learning. We wanted to understand the challenges in literacy both from the perspective of teachers and as experienced by pupils, particularly those identified as underachieving in literacy, across the school. We also wanted to get a feel for the home background of pupils by involving parents. We anticipated that our holistic approach to the research question, within the overall collaborative inquiry framework (Bray *et al.*, 2000), would lead us to reflect on ways of improving the rate of achievement among boys.

The initial visit to the school helped us to prepare a basic research plan which included details of the possible sample, methods, a timeframe and the nature of the data to be collected. The timelines were set in collaboration with the school team.

We aimed to prepare a descriptive and insightful case study on the school in relation to our research question. While we chose a mixed method approach, our particular focus was on qualitative methods to help us in eliciting and capturing the emotional experience of children in relation to literacy and writing. Our initial sample included teachers, target group children and parents of target group children.

This was, however, an open and flexible schedule. We incorporated changes in the sample and the research design in response to unfolding circumstances. For example, we decided not to interview parents given our time constraints. Similarly, we included members of the students' school council to incorporate views of a representative group of children about their experiences, to contrast and complement the experience of the target group of children, whose progress and perspectives we analysed in greater detail. School council members were children from different year groups and, in fact, included some of our target group members. Our sample is demonstrated in Table 12.1.

Data collection

Our team had only five working days, spread over six working weeks, to conduct the main inquiry. (We used the other five days to plan, prepare and analyse our data, and to report back to the school.) Of course, the fact that there were four of us meant that this was a total of 20 days of fieldwork.

Bearing the tight timeline in mind, we decided to design a short initial questionnaire for teachers, conduct interviews with a target group of individual children and with the inclusion coordinator, and facilitate a focus group discussion with members of the school council. Mrs Harris distributed the questionnaires to the class teachers. She also sent out letters to parents to seek their permission for the participation of their children in the inquiry. This was an invaluable help to the team as we only made weekly visits to the school.

We felt that it was important to understand the challenges that children were experiencing in classes. With this in mind, we began by observing literacy classes in different year groups, working as pairs of researchers. This helped us to establish reliability and validity of our observations. In addition, we collected documentary evidence in the form of samples of writing produced by the target group of children. We also referred to the entries that teachers made in their routine written records. At the same time, we interviewed teachers about the nature of the problems that students faced in literacy and how teachers assist students in overcoming these difficulties.

Table 12.1 Research participants

Sample	Size of sample
Inclusion coordinator	1
Teachers	6
Children from school council	8
Children in target group	11

This methodological triangulation helped us in obtaining a coherent picture of the issue being researched.

The different methods used in the inquiry and the purposes they served towards fulfilling our research objective are outlined in Table 12.2.

The views of children

Conducting an inquiry with children was an integral and challenging part of the process. In particular, careful planning was necessary to engage children in the inquiry process and to understand the issue of underachievement from their perspective.

As a team, we were more culturally diverse than the group of learners in the study. The diversity of our experiences and cultural backgrounds brought richness and creativity to the research process (Bray *et al.*, 2000; Mealman and Lawrence, 2002). The learners were of white British and African origin. We were aware that they may not have wanted to talk about their writing, so we began to think of innovative ways of establishing a rapport with them. Our main priority was to make them feel comfortable with us and to respond candidly to our questions.

We developed a game which required the learners to join up letters of the alphabet in different ways to form a word (see Figure 12.1). This was designed as an ice-breaker, to be used before each individual interview. The purpose was to make the sad, lonely letters of the alphabet happy by finding friends for them and making them into words. This proved to be a really helpful starting point as it directed each child's attention to literacy. At the same time, it introduced the concept of emotion and feelings. This led us easily on to the interview questions about their own feelings about writing. Since we were from different cultural backgrounds, we also needed time to adjust to

Table 12.2 A summary of research methods

Research methods	Purpose
• Classroom observations • Teachers questionnaire • Individual interviews with children • Samples of children's writing with teacher's feedback on them • Teachers' diary notes.	To identify the problems that learners face

a. Target group
  • picture-elicitation (see Figure 12.1)
  • children's diaries (see Figure 12.2)
  • individual interviews.
b. Other children
  • focus group discussion.
	To explore children's experiences of writing
	a. target group children
	b. other children.

These letters feel so lonely in this empty page. Could you please make them feel important? Use them in any way you prefer (e.g. colour, draw, make a word . . .).

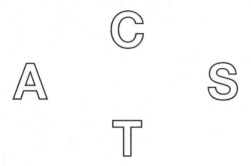

Figure 12.1 Ice-breaker game used to develop a rapport with individual children during the interviews.

each child's temperament and their strong local accents, and enable them to adjust to our many different ways of speaking English.

Two team members participated in each interview session. While one talked to the child, the other made detailed notes of the responses. This allowed the interviewer to focus on the questions. The person taking notes in the interview was seated at a distance, so that the child did not feel overwhelmed by so many adults. Two sets of interviews were conducted simultaneously in the same room, so that the children did not feel that they were being singled out.

In addition, we used a diary to capture the emotional experiences of children in literacy classes (see Figure 12.2). We created this diary page and distributed multiple copies to the class teachers of the target students. The diary page was to be filled in by children with the class teachers' help, after each language writing task conducted in the class over the period of one week.

We facilitated focus group discussions with school council members based on some of the common themes emerging from the interviews of target group children. These were recorded and also two members made detailed notes of the discussion as back up for the electronic recording. These multiple approaches to gathering information helped us address the complexity of capturing the emotional experience of children more effectively (Cohen *et al.*, 2003).

Collaborating with the school

Mrs Harris played multiple roles during the course of our research. She was our gatekeeper to access different staff members and her status as the

Inclusion Standard Diary Sheet

Name: _____

What have you been writing?

Did you enjoy this?

☐ Yes   ☐ No

Why?

Please draw . . .

```
┌─────────────────────────────────────────┐
│                                         │
│                                         │
│                                         │
│                                         │
└─────────────────────────────────────────┘
```

How did you feel about this?

☺   😐   ☹

Figure 12.2 Sample of diary page handed out to the class teachers to be filled in by the students identified as underachieving in writing.

inclusion coordinator and member of the school's senior management team, gave her authority within the school setting. This also meant that not only did she provide us with access to human resources, but to material resources as well. This included photocopying facilities and materials for interviews, documentary evidence about the school and children's work, a room in which we could conduct interviews and relax, and access the Internet.

Providing Mrs Harris with a scheduled plan of our visits enabled her to secure the necessary resources when they were needed. This included providing us with the code for the photocopier and library space in which we could work. She even arranged for us to have a laptop with Internet access so that we could work on our presentation on the school premises.

While these may seem to be minor issues, having such resources where we could all work together as a team was really helpful. Given our different academic commitments, we would have struggled to arrange to spend time together on other occasions, and with such facilities. This logistical support reflected Mrs Harris's understanding of the research process which involves spending a great deal of time organising and analysing the data. She was also aware of our timelines for handing in the presentations and the coursework. She was so supportive that she often anticipated some of the challenges in advance, and asked us what we might need during our next visit to the school.

In addition to being the gatekeeper and facilitator of the inquiry process, Mrs Harris was also a key informant in the research. Given her years of experience in the school, she was knowledgeable about the various aspects of the school, and supplied the information we required.

In all these ways, Mrs Harris played an active part in the research process by being our supporter and critical friend. Having recently completed a Master's degree herself, she was supportive of the inquiry in practical ways. As we discussed possible ways of conducting the research, and what methods to use, she commented on the feasibility of our plans, given the time available with teachers and students. She discussed the progress of the work with us at the end of each visit, so kept close tabs on the inquiry process, while at the same time, allowed us to take the lead. Her feedback and inputs helped in streamlining the focus of the inquiry and in keeping the process on track from beginning to end. A 'shared commitment to the inquiry question' (Bray *et al.*, 2000: 11) from the school as well as the team of researchers ensured that a rigorous and persistently reflective stance was taken towards the inquiry process. At the same time, relationships were developed and maintained between the team members as well as with school staff, which facilitated the inquiry process to progress smoothly and led to productive outcomes (Bray *et al.*, 2000; Mealman and Lawrence, 2002).

More generally, our team felt very welcome in the school community. During our visits, we were able to use the staffroom space to keep our bags, discuss, relax and make tea and coffee, and use other kitchen facilities available for staff. The school was not obliged to offer us these facilities, but it was a gesture we appreciated and was much respected by our team.

Spending time in the staffroom during our visits was also helpful in providing time for a quick catch up with the teachers whose classes we had observed. While this aspect of our observation did not feed directly into our research, it helped us to get a feel for the ethos of the school. It also gave us an insight into what we saw as the warm and caring relationships among staff members.

Working as a team

An important aspect of our team's work was the establishing of ground rules, which we reviewed as we went along. Basically, there were two rules: to accommodate the needs of each group member; and for individuals to complete tasks for which they had assumed responsibility.

Temperamentally, we were very different from one other. Anna was always perceived to be the most critical, often dismissive in her attitude. She was quiet but intense in her approach. Zoa, with her teaching background, added a practical dimension to the issue being discussed. She would always be the first one to document the inquiry process, and encouraged us to develop a kind of group think tank. It was her job to be the contact person, since she was from the UK and was most able to communicate easily with the school. Having one person as a point of contact was helpful in keeping the channels of communication clear and precise, and so avoiding any duplication or confusion.

Irene was light-hearted and carefree, yet seemed the most eager to learn. Despite her limited experience in school settings, she was enthusiastic about the research and compensated for her lack of experience through hard work and commitment. I identified most with Irene because we were both part-time members of the Master's course. Drawing on my experience of conducting research, I encouraged the group members to be reflective. As a result we constantly drew on our previous experiences and our exposure to literature to inform our decisions.

While Zoa's familiarity with the English education system was an asset to the team, we benefitted from suggestions made by Mrs Harris who had an insider understanding of the context. While we were not able to commit additional time for team building, we travelled to and from the school together and shared meals. This gave us time to get to know each other better and share some light moments together. This enabled us to present ourselves as a 'team' to the school, rather than just a group of individual students.

Each team member had been exposed to different systems of learning, and so many issues had to be debated. For example, we all had a different understanding of how to analyse the mechanics of written English in the samples of the boys' writing. After much debate, we decided to follow the approach to grammar used in the English school system. We also debated the way we should organise the seating for individual or group interviews. Some team members viewed it from the point of view of a teacher, suggesting that the children should be seated at the other side of the table, while others favoured the more informal approach of seating the children next to the researchers to allow them to be more comfortable.

As the inquiry progressed, we found ourselves more and more committed to the group task. We respected each other's different view points, and spent many hours discussing challenges until we reached a decision that was acceptable to everyone. One key example of teamwork was preparing the group presentation of our findings, both at the university and to the senior management team at the school. We discussed the various sections and what should be covered under each heading. Given her intense nature and critical eye, Anna volunteered to put together the slides on data analysis. Irene volunteered to prepare the slides on methodology, while Zoa, based on her background in schools and teaching, decided to focus on preparing the background information on the school and the research issue at hand. Having had wider research experience than other members in the group, I volunteered to focus on reflective aspects of the research and the group work. Finally, Zoa volunteered to put together all the slides, given her proficiency with IT, and this was shared with the whole group. We then worked together on the slides and saw it all coming together as a coherent whole. This could have been a challenge if some of us had had conflicting interests. However, just as in other tasks, what seemed to guide us was the need to play to our strengths and to build on our group discussions. This required an experience of shared power in the group tasks and an absence of internal competition (Mealman and Lawrence, 2002).

Concluding thoughts

We saw St Anthony's School as a key stakeholder in our research and wanted to make sure that everybody would gain from our involvement. This meant that the development of good working relationships and channels of communication were essential to the success of our work. Put simply, if nobody in the school was prepared to take notice of our findings, our efforts would be wasted.

As I have explained, Mrs Harris was a key factor in this respect. Her association with our team provided us with credibility as researchers within the school setting. Specifically, it ensured that other members of the school staff were open to our questions and inquisitiveness, and supported our work whenever we sought their assistance for carrying out a research task.

Schools are busy places and it is necessary for those involved to make space for external groups of researchers so their involvement becomes meaningful. For us, the staff's active involvement in the research process and genuine interest in the findings of our research proved to be a great motivator. Feeling valued and respected by the school helped to sustain our commitment to the process.

We sensed that the staff noticed our behaviour and expected a degree of professionalism and responsiveness towards their school culture and ethos. We carried the additional responsibility of representing the university. Moreover, we were part of a process of on-going collaboration that went beyond our coursework. All of this became a conscious part of our identity as student researchers while, at the same time, helping to enhance our credibility.

In a way that I had not anticipated, the project provided us with an opportunity to deepen our theoretical understanding about educational inclusion in an English context by giving us direct experience of practice. At the same time, there was an opportunity for the school to gain from the research activity and outcomes, and work towards improving the participation and achievement of the boys based on the evidence generated by the research.

Finally, for me personally, the engagement with the school opened up opportunities for further collaboration and research, as I was given permission to conduct the pilot study for my doctoral research on leadership and inclusion. This involved shadowing the head teacher, a research method that would have been difficult to use in an unfamiliar setting.

References

Ainscow, M., Booth T. and Dyson, A. (2006) *Improving Schools, Developing Inclusion*. London: Routledge.

Bray, J. N., Lee, J., Smith L. L. and Yorks, L. (2000) *Collaborative Inquiry in Practice: Action, Reflection, and Meaning Making*. London: Sage.

Cohen, L., Manion, L. and Morrison K. (2003) *Research Methods in Education*. London: RoutledgeFalmer.

Jones, S. and Myhill, D. (2004a) 'Seeing things differently: teachers' constructions of underachievement'. *Gender and Education*, 16(4): 531–546.

Jones, S. and Myhill, D (2004b) '"Troublesome boys" and "compliant girls": gender identity and perceptions of achievement and underachievement'. *British Journal of Sociology of Education*, 25(5): 547–561.

Mealman, C. A. and Lawrence, R. L. (2002) *Reflective Synergy: A Research Model for Collaborative Inquiry*. Paper presented at the 43rd Annual Meeting of the Adult Education Research Conference, Raleigh, NC, 24–26 May 2002. Raleigh, NC: North Carolina State University. Available at: http://www.nl.edu/academics/cas/ace/upload/Reflective-syn.pdf (accessed on 30 June 2009).

Moore, M., Ainscow, M. and Fox, S. (2007) *The Manchester Inclusion Standard*. Manchester: Manchester City Council.

Smith, E. (2003) 'Failing boys and moral panics: perspectives on the underachievement debate'. *British Journal of Educational Studies*, 51(3): 282–295.

UNESCO (1994) *The Salamanca Statement and Framework for Action on Special Needs Education*. Paris: UNESCO.

Conclusion

Learning through inquiry

Susie Miles and Mel Ainscow

> The accounts provided in this book focus on ways in which education practitioners can respond positively and imaginatively to learner diversity. They illustrate the use of an inquiry-based approach that involves analysing contexts, making interruptions and creating conversations. Reflecting on the experience of developing and using this approach, the concluding chapter presents a series of propositions for developing more effective ways of conducting inquiries and responding to learner diversity in schools.

The approach we have presented is based on the assumption that *schools know more than they use*, but that much of this knowledge is tacit and unexplored. A key challenge for schools, therefore, is to identify this underused expertise. However, it is not enough simply to identify this knowledge – we also need to learn how to move it around, within and between schools, so as to develop new, more effective ways of reaching those learners who are currently not being reached.

As we have explained, there are difficulties in making this happen, not least because the expertise of teachers, and other support staff, is largely unarticulated. In order to access this reservoir of unused expertise, it is necessary to create a common language of practice that will facilitate reflection, mutual challenge and the sharing of ideas.

The research we summarised in the Introduction has shown how evidence can provide the stimulus for the development of such a language of practice in a way that can create a catalyst for change. Specifically, evidence can help to create space for reappraisal and rethinking by interrupting existing discourses, practices and beliefs, and by focusing attention on new ways of working and responding to diversity.

All of this involves processes of social learning within specific contexts. It requires new thinking and, indeed, new relationships that promote active connections among learners and practitioners. As we have seen through the accounts in this book, such collaboration within the workplace is socially complex. There is, therefore, a need for forms of leadership that encourage the trust, mutual understanding and shared values and behaviours that can bind colleagues together, and make cooperative action and inquiry possible.

In this final chapter, then, we reflect on the accounts provided by our colleagues in order to suggest practical guidance for using an inquiry-based approach to diversity in schools. In so doing, we keep in mind the following questions posed in the Introduction: What kinds of practices might help schools reach out to all of their learners? How can such practices be developed? How can we ensure that such practices are of high quality, inclusive in the broadest possible sense and respectful of diversity? How can learners themselves play a greater role in improving the educational experience for all? What methods of inquiry need to be developed to promote more relevant forms of research? And what role can school-based inquiry play in stimulating and even initiating change?

Using an inquiry-based approach

It is noticeable that many of the inquiries presented in this book adopted a student voice approach. These voices, which have been truly diverse and challenging, have included: listening to and challenging students' views of mental illness; exploring the experience of being bullied and marginalised in large secondary schools; using photography to better understand the communication barriers faced by a child using a communication aid in a primary school; and using drawing to elicit the career aspirations of primary school students who speak English as an additional language.

The authors of the chapters are themselves an extremely diverse group – most are experienced teachers, while others are in the early stages of a research career. Although their life experiences are many and varied, they all share a passion for learners who experience marginalisation and have turned to research to discover new ways forward. So, for example, the experience of being a parent of two disabled daughters was the stimulus for Clare Millington to become a student again; Hannah Scott's interest in learner empowerment was influenced by difficulties she experienced as a child in school; and, concerned by the poor practice witnessed in care homes, Zoe O'Riordan returned to education to explore the possible reasons for this and to do something about it.

Although we are recommending an overall approach to conducting school-based inquiries, each chapter describes a unique way of working, developed in response to an analysis of the particular context. In each inquiry the formulation of clear research questions, encapsulating the problem identified, was critical to the success of the process.

A predominant approach to the collecting of evidence from students themselves was through the use of various visual methods, and this involved a great deal of imagination and courage on behalf of the researchers. In the project reported in Chapter 10, for example, students were asked to draw their career aspirations, while, in Chapter 4, we read how photographs were used to record and later reflect upon, and further explore, places and spaces in the school environment. Inspired by participatory photography principles, Emma Lindley (Chapter 9) developed her own unique approach to stimulating discussions among young people about mental illness, which she has called the 'photo-vignette' technique. The combination of a striking photo and a few carefully formulated sentences led to the challenging and exploration of preconceptions and stereotypes in carefully managed focus groups.

Although the authors have talked a great deal about the mechanics of conducting an inquiry in school environments, the chapters also touch upon key challenges to the development of more inclusive practices in education, such as: the importance of developing good relationships between students, and between students and those who teach them; the necessity of communicating clearly at all times; and the difficulties faced on a daily basis in maintaining good relationships and communicating clearly, given the considerable time pressures in schools. Despite such difficulties, the links between research and action are strong in all the inquiries, even though the potential for bringing about actual change varies considerably between the contexts.

A device which most of the authors used was the reflective research diary. In Chapter 11, Malcolm Williams and Zoe O'Riordan used diaries to good effect by presenting their sometimes opposing views of the inquiry process, given their respective insider and outsider status. Indeed, they conclude by saying that in a future collaborative inquiry, it is with the sensitive management of the imbalance of power between researchers that they would begin.

Working propositions

Reflecting on these experiences has led us to formulate working propositions, which we suggest can guide initiatives aimed at strengthening responses to diversity in schools. We describe them as 'working' propositions to underline their provisional status. That is to say, we reserve the right to refine them in the light of further experiences. All we are saying at this stage is that these statements represent the best advice we feel able to offer – both to ourselves in carrying out further school-based research, and to others who wish to use this approach. Central to these propositions is our conviction that difference, although a social construction, can be a resource and a stimulus for change, rather than a problem or a drain on resources.

Our five working propositions are as follows:

1 Make use of existing expertise.

2 Create conversations about practice.
3 Use evidence as the catalyst for change.
4 Strengthen collaboration.
5 Adopt forms of leadership that encourage a spirit of inquiry.

In what follows we explain these ideas in detail and explore their implications for practice in the field.

Proposition 1: Make use of existing expertise

In simple terms, *diversity* in education refers to self-evident differences between children and young people. These include differences in attainment, gender, ethnic background, family and social background, interests and aptitudes, social skills, amongst many others. However, it is our contention that understanding difference is far from straightforward.

So, for example, the notion that learners can be categorised in terms of their social class, their access to particular linguistic codes or their 'intelligence', has changed to take account of more recent concerns with 'social exclusion'. This, in turn, has generated other forms of categorisation, focusing, for example, on children in public care, traveller children, disabled children and children from particular ethnic groups – all of whom are perceived to be at risk of being marginalised from educational opportunities and encountering barriers to learning.

Understandings of difference in education may change over time, but they also vary between cultural contexts, whether that be at the national level, or at the level of particular institutions (Artiles and Dyson, 2005). The implications of all of this are: that difference in the school population is not so much identified as constructed; that attention paid to groups of learners who are perceived to be different will vary according to the time in history and the context; that these forms of difference are understood, and explained, in particular ways; and that implications for policy and practice flow from these constructions (Ainscow *et al.*, 2007).

Our approach starts from this view that diversity is socially constructed. As we explained in the Introduction, it is also informed by the work of Robinson (1998), who suggests that practices are activities that solve problems in particular situations. This means that to explain a practice is to reveal the problem for which it serves as a solution. So, in working closely with practitioners in developing responses to learner differences, we have found that we can make inferences about how school staff have 'constructed' the issue of diversity and the assumptions that are involved in the decisions made. We have also observed how initial formulations are sometimes rethought as a result of an engagement with various forms of evidence.

In all the contexts described in this book we see examples of how evidence can stimulate such rethinking. The accounts also reveal knowledge, expertise and creativity within schools that can be mobilised in order to develop a greater capacity for involving all children and young people in learning. Logically, therefore, the starting point is with what already exists. In other words, the overriding strategic aim must be to analyse what goes on in classrooms, around schools and in children's lives in order to identify those barriers that are making it difficult for some students to participate and learn, and the resources that can be used to address these barriers.

As we have seen, when such an analysis is carried out, it usually reveals different types of barriers. The studies described in this book focus on contextual barriers – in contrast to the traditional deficit view, where barriers are assumed to be located *within* the child, or in their home background. Elsewhere we have described this way of thinking as an *inclusive turn* (Ainscow *et al.*, 2007). This involves moving away from explanations of educational failure that concentrate on the characteristics of individual children and their families, towards an analysis of the barriers to participation and learning experienced by students within schools (Booth and Ainscow, 2002). This means that it is essential to seek the views of those students whose 'voices' may not have previously been listened to, since they are not responding to existing educational arrangements.

With appropriate support, these previously overlooked groups of children can be encouraged to participate in the improvement of schools (Ainscow, 1999). It is, therefore, hardly surprising that an overarching theme which emerges from all the chapters is that of listening to and consulting with students. However, just as teachers' knowledge is rarely articulated, the same is true of students' ideas and experience. Their views are often overlooked because they tend not to be considered important, and sometimes they are consulted in a tokenistic way (Fielding, 2001).

In some instances, the barriers that are revealed may be physical in nature, and related to access to particular classroom resources, areas of a school or even the curriculum itself. The barriers which are often most difficult to overcome, however, are those in the minds of adults, where the limitations set by previous professional experiences, or by perceptions of learners from certain types of backgrounds, can lead to low expectations of particular groups of young people.

We see this vividly in Chapter 4, where an inquiry into the effectiveness of a communication aid, from the point of view of a non-verbal child, leads to some important challenges about the tendency of teachers to ask questions of the same confident and competent children, so avoiding those who struggle to give the desired answers in the required time. The account also highlights the dangers inherent in a highly skilled teaching assistant becoming the spokesperson for a child with complex needs. In this way, the strong focus on pupil voice and perspectives led to a much wider discussion about classroom practices and organisation.

The evidence collected by and from young people whose secondary school experience had been so negative (reported in Chapter 3), indicates that this was due to a breakdown in their relationship with adults. They reported that their teachers had not acted swiftly enough in response to their reports of being bullied, or of facing severe difficulties at home.

The implication of all of this is that attempts to develop responses to learner diversity have to be mainly inwards-looking, since the solutions to problems identified through school-based inquiries can almost certainly be found within the human and physical resources of the existing school. We see a good example of this in Chapter 6, where we read of how older children in a primary school take a lead in the inquiry as 'ambassadors', exploring ways in which very young children could participate in the school council. The answer lay within the schoolchildren themselves.

Such approaches require education practitioners to reflect on their own ways of working, take risks with the involvement of pupils themselves and explore child-friendly ways of engaging all stakeholders. This is a simple point but it is fundamental to the rationale of this book. As we have argued, schools know more than they use, but they often need the stimulus of an inquiry – sometimes involving outsiders – in order to identify and so make better use of available expertise.

With this central idea in mind, our work has involved a search for forms of school-based inquiry that: have the flexibility to deal with the uniqueness of particular educational occurrences and contexts; allow schools and classrooms to be understood from the perspectives of different participants, not least children themselves; and encourage stakeholders to investigate their own situations and practices with a view to bringing about improvements (e.g. Ainscow, 1999; Ainscow *et al.*, 2006). It has involved the development of a form of collaborative *action research*, an approach to inquiry that in its original form sought to use the experimental approach of social science with programmes of social action in response to social problems (Lewin, 1946). More recently action research has come to refer to a process of inquiry undertaken by practitioners in their own workplaces (Armstrong and Moore, 2004; Elliott, 1991; O'Hanlon, 2003). Here the aim is to improve practice and understanding through a combination of systematic reflection and strategic innovation.

Action research is sometimes dismissed as not being 'proper' research by those working within more traditional research paradigms. Others, while acknowledging it as a worthwhile activity for practitioners, are anxious that claims for the validity of findings should not be made beyond the particular contexts in which the investigation is carried out (e.g. Hammersley, 1992). Proponents of action research, on the other hand, have responded to these criticisms by rejecting the conceptions of rigour imposed by traditional social science, and by mounting their own counter-criticism of the methodology and assumptions about knowledge upon which these conceptions of rigour are dependent (e.g. Winter, 1989). They claim, for example, that the notions of rigour to which many researchers aspire are oppressive, restrictive and prescriptive, designed to perpetuate the hierarchical divisions between the producers and users of research (Iano, 1986).

In devising a suitable methodology we have been aware of others who have attempted to follow a similar path. For example, Poplin and Weeres (1992) report a study called Voices From the Inside, carried out by students, teachers, administrators and parents in four schools in the USA. Here the aim was to create strategies that allowed everyone in the school to speak and ensured that everyone be heard. Thus, the research allowed all participants to be both the researchers and, at the same time, the subjects of the research. Since the study began with the assumption that academics had already misnamed the problems of schooling, the roles of outsiders had to be rethought so that those on the inside could come to know and articulate the problems they experience. The use of this process was reported to have led to many changes in the schools, although it was also found to be extremely time-consuming.

The inclusive research reported by Hannah Scott in Chapter 8 has a rather similar orientation. It took place over an 18-month period and enabled young people with learning difficulties to play a key role in reflecting upon their own experience as learners, as well as taking a lead as co-researchers. The adoption of the role of researcher by the students with learning difficulties was a major challenge to the attitudes of the teaching and support staff of the further education college, forcing them to rethink their own attitudes to disability.

From our earlier experiences of research with schools, we have found it useful to take account of four principles as we seek to involve practitioners in processes of research. These are that they should: 'be of direct help to people in the contexts involved; inform the development of policies and practices elsewhere; demonstrate rigour such that the findings are worthy of wider attention; and inform the thinking of the "outsider" research team' (Stubbs, 1995: 41–42).

In adopting this socially responsible approach to research, we have become clearer about both the advantages and, of course, the difficulties involved in carrying out school-based development and research projects. In terms of advantages, there was strong evidence that the practitioners involved often found the process to be both informative and stimulating. Specifically, they found that the need to engage with multiple interpretations of events forced them to think much more deeply about their own perceptions. Furthermore, exploring ways of valuing points of view that they might usually ignore, or even oppose, also seemed to stimulate them to consider previously ignored possibilities for the development of thinking and practice. At the same time they found the process to be affirming, giving them an opportunity to celebrate many achievements in their working contexts.

These earlier experiences highlighted some of the problems that can occur when practitioners take on the task of carrying out what might be referred to as *insider* research. We found, for example, that despite a commitment to reporting a wide range of opinions, some accounts revealed little evidence of alternative voices, thus giving the impression of what seemed to be a most unlikely level of consensus. Sometimes there was very little evidence presented from children and parents, gaps that seem particularly regrettable when we read the findings of the Poplin and Weeres' study, reported earlier. Finally, there remain concerns about confidentiality. Specifically, as the accounts are read by more people in a particular context, can we be sure that the views of certain individuals will remain anonymous?

What is encouraging about the collection of accounts presented here is that, in most cases, learners were consulted as a matter of course, rather than as an afterthought, or a tokenistic box-ticking exercise. In some of the inquiries, young people's views on a range of topics (for example, school attendance in Chapter 3 and staff selection in Chapter 11) were elicited using a number of imaginative techniques; whereas in others, the young people played a central role: conducting peer interviews in Chapter 3; being 'ambassadors' in Chapter 6. Six-year-old boys and girls were selected in the project reported in Chapter 7 to pioneer an approach to behaviour management and task completion – one particular girl demonstrated maturity beyond her years in responding in a consistently positive manner to a boy who was at risk of disciplinary exclusion.

What is noticeably missing from this collection are the views of parents and community members. An effort was made in the inquiry described in Chapter 10 to engage with parents' aspirations for their children's careers, but this proved challenging due to the considerable communication difficulties faced in the school.

Coincidentally, a group on our M.Ed course is currently conducting an inquiry into parent unwillingness to engage with their children's primary school experience. One of the major challenges is that the parents whom the researchers most want to interview are those who are least likely to set foot in the school. The inquiry team is exploring ways of meeting parents on neutral territory, possibly in their homes. They are also trying to engage parents who have positive attitudes to the school by encouraging them to act as 'ambassadors' and help them make contact with parents who seem to be disaffected, probably due to their own negative school experiences. This process is, of course, fraught with logistical and ethical difficulties.

Overall then, the methodology described here can be characterised as a process of social learning. As we have explained, this requires a group of stakeholders within a school to engage in a search for a common agenda to guide their inquiries and, at much the same time, a series of struggles to establish ways of working that enable them to collect and find meaning in different types of information. All of this has to be carried out in a way that will be of direct benefit to those in the contexts under consideration. In so doing, the members of the group are exposed to manifestations of one another's perspectives and assumptions. At its best, all of this provides wonderful opportunities for developing new understandings. However, such possibilities can only be utilised if potential social, cultural, linguistic and micro-political barriers are overcome.

The inquiry reported by Abha Sandill (in Chapter 12) provides a striking example of such mutual learning, where the diversity of the student group was in itself seen as a focus for learning for the school staff, while at the same time the key member of staff in the school, who had recently gained a Master's degree, provided logistical support and engaged in critically reflective discussions with the team. In other words, the inquiry was seen as a major contribution to school practice, rather than an onerous intrusion.

This reminds us of the traditional gap between research and practice, such that practitioners rarely engage with or benefit from research processes and findings. We believe that our approach to school-based inquiries can help to close this gap. As Robinson (1998) notes, it has generally been assumed that the gap has resulted from inadequate dissemination strategies. The implication being that educational research *does* speak to issues of practice, if only the right people would listen. She suggests an alternative explanation, pointing out that research findings may well continue to be ignored, regardless of how well they are communicated, because they bypass the ways in which practitioners formulate the problems they face and deal with the constraints within which they have to work.

Yet, as we have seen, when practitioners and pupils are key players in the inquiry process, the potential benefits are enormous, not least in that the understandings gained can have an immediate impact on the development of thinking and practice. At the same time, we do not wish to suggest that participatory research is free of difficulties. On the contrary, it can be time-consuming, deeply disturbing and potentially life changing. Indeed, we have received many phone calls from distressed student researchers who have faced major logistical and ethical dilemmas in schools for which there have been no easy or straightforward solutions.

Sometimes they also struggle with cross-cultural misunderstandings within their own research team, which only they can resolve. Nevertheless, it helps them to be able talk through these dilemmas with a more experienced researcher. Engagement in a school-based inquiry demands more time and energy than an equivalent Master's level course (see Appendix), yet students claim to have learned so much more by carrying out a piece of real-world research. It is an experience which leads to deep, rather than superficial, learning.

Proposition 2: Create conversations about practice

The inquiries reported in this book were influenced by earlier research carried out by members of our Manchester team. In particular, they were informed by the experiences of the collaborative action research network Understanding and Developing Inclusive Practices in Schools, described in the Introduction (see Ainscow *et al.*, 2006, for a detailed account of this research). Together, over a period of three years, the partners in the network explored ways of developing more inclusive practices in the schools by investigating the barriers experienced and the methods used to overcome these barriers.

In terms of the development of a methodology for enabling research to contribute to more equitable policy and practice, the main lessons were:

- It is possible to infuse a critical dimension into a collaborative action research project, so that issues of social justice (in this case, a focus on inclusion) are considered as practitioners shape their action.
- The critical friendship of *outsiders* (in this case, university researchers) is a way of keeping these issues on the agenda. Such engagement is capable of bringing about significant changes in practitioner thinking, which is, in turn, reflected in changes in practice.
- Where such changes take place, it is useful to think of them as the result of an 'interruption' to continuing practice which brings about a transformation from 'single-loop' to 'double-loop' learning (Argyris and Schön, 1996); that is, from learning which enables practice to be improved incrementally to learning which shifts the assumptions on which practice is based.

We also learned some of the problems inherent in this way of working. For instance:

- Although transformations in thinking and practice occurred, they were far from universal. Some practitioners and their schools continued in their established course with little deviation.
- Although we understood *inclusion* as a broad social justice issue, some practitioners interpreted it in rather narrow terms – for instance, as being about improving the attainments of low-attaining students. Because we did not offer practitioners a robust model of inclusion as a set of principles on which practice could be based, we were very much in the hands of teacher interpretations.
- In time, the research process generated a model of inclusive practice. However, this was at a generalised level. It did not form the basis for any impact on policy, and, as it stood, was not readily transferable to other contexts.

The most significant outcome of the work of the network was the way it demonstrated how an engagement with various forms of evidence can create a sense of interruption to existing ways of thinking and working within a school. We found, too, that, under certain conditions, such interruptions can stimulate self-questioning, creativity and action. In so doing, they can sometimes lead to a reframing of perceived problems that, in turn, draws attention to overlooked possibilities for addressing barriers to participation and learning.

This led us to conclude that at the heart of the processes in schools where changes in practice do occur is the development of a common language with which colleagues can talk to one another and, indeed, to themselves about detailed aspects of their practice. Without such a language teachers find it difficult to experiment with new possibilities. Much of what teachers do during the intensive classroom encounters that occur is carried out at an automatic, intuitive level – there is little time to stop and think. This is why having opportunities to keep reflective diaries (see Chapter 10) and discuss aspects of practice are so crucial to the success of attempts to create inclusive opportunities for learners.

It is through such shared experiences that colleagues can help one another to articulate what they currently do and define what they might like to do. It is also the means of creating space, in which taken-for-granted assumptions about particular groups of learners can be subjected to mutual critique – as demonstrated in Chapter 8 where assumptions about disability were challenged through inclusive research.

We conclude, therefore, that a methodology for developing more inclusive practices must take account of the social processes of learning that go on within particular schools. As we have argued, this requires groups of stakeholders to look for a common agenda to guide their discussions of practice and, at the same time, engage in a series of struggles to establish ways of working that will enable them to collect and find meaning in different types of information.

However, as we explained in the Introduction, none of this provides a straightforward mechanism for the development of more inclusive practices and any space for reflection that is created as a result of engaging with evidence may be filled according to conflicting agendas.

So, what needs to be done to move forward? First of all, those who manage and lead schools have to be given the space and authority to carry out an analysis of their contexts in order to develop improvement stategies that are relevant. Then, there are the strategic challenges that need to be addressed, not least that of finding time.

Consequently, as we noted in the Introduction, it is necessary to explore ways of developing the capacity of those within schools to reveal and challenge deeply entrenched deficit views of difference, which define certain types of students as 'lacking something' (Trent et al., 1998). This involves being vigilant in scrutinising how deficit assumptions may be influencing perceptions of certain students.

Sometimes when we talk to head teachers and senior staff in schools about the need for staff to collect and engage with evidence, they respond by saying that they see the point, but that there is simply no time to do this in the school day. We disagree. Time is the currency we use in schools to signal that something is important. Although the lack of time is frequently an excuse, when something is seen as important, time is almost always found. Our argument continues that our experience tells us that to improve the learning of its students a school must invest in the learning of the staff. And, as we have illustrated in this book, evidence collected within a school can be a powerful stimulus to such professional learning.

Proposition 3: Use evidence as the catalyst for change

When collecting evidence in school settings, strategic questions are crucial in determining what information is needed and how it should be collected. This is the case in any kind of research enterprise. A key feature of the approach that we are recommending is that these questions must be generated by practitioners themselves, in order to ensure that the focus is on real-world issues and that the findings of the investigations will be meaningful and relevant.

Hopkins (2008) explains that research questions can be located on a continuum where at one end they can be tightly focused (when it is known exactly what information is required), while at the other end questions can be broader and more open. The investigations that are needed in order to address diversity in schools are usually exploratory. A broad agenda is developed based on the informed 'hunches' of those carrying out the inquiry, and the questions are likely to be open in nature. As information is collected and considered, the questions can gradually become more focused.

The choice of possible research methods for such inquiries is limitless – it is the research questions that are crucial in determining which methods to use. At the same time, it is important to remember that all research methods have their strengths and limitations. So, for example, statistical information is often an excellent starting point for an inquiry.

Large quantities of statistical information are now available in schools regarding attendance, behaviour and student performance. In recent years the extent and sophistication of such data have improved, so much so that the progress of groups and individuals can now be tracked in considerable detail, giving a much greater sense of the value that a school is adding to its students. If necessary, further relevant statistical material can be collected through questionnaire surveys of the views of students, staff members and, where relevant, parents and carers.

However, of itself, statistical information tells us very little. What brings data to life is when *insiders* start to scrutinise and ask questions as to their significance, bringing detailed experiences and knowledge to bear on the process of interpretation. Even then, there are still limitations that need to be kept in mind. Statistics provide patterns of what exists: they tell us what things are like but give little understanding as to why things are as they are, or how they came to be like that. This is why methodological experts tend to promote the idea of using mixed research methods (e.g. Robson, 2002). It is also why evidence collected through qualitative approaches is needed to supplement statistical data. More specifically, qualitative research methods can help us to address 'how' and 'why' questions, in order to determine what action needs to be taken to initiate change in a school.

As we have seen in the inquiries described in this book, qualitative research methods can take many forms. When used effectively, they can help us to develop a deeper understanding of the way participants within schools and classrooms construct meaning about their experiences. The forms of data captured, in all the inquiries we have presented, revealed insider perceptions and knowledge.

Observation of one kind or another is almost always a necessary element of attempts to investigate educational processes. Again, this can take different forms, depending on the nature of the research questions. So, for example, observations may be guided by a relatively focused set of indicators or, at the other extreme, by a series of open questions or themes. In addition, unexpected events can reveal something of significance to the inquiry.

Learning how to observe within classrooms and in a school environment is a challenge – there is always a great deal going on, and it is easy to become distracted (useful guidance is provided in Hopkins, 2008). Sometimes it helps to make video recordings – although, again, there are advantages and limitations to this method of data recording. It is useful to be able to replay the recording in order to look at sections in more detail, and it is good for groups of colleagues to discuss a video recording. On the other hand, the video camera can only record what is within the frame and important events may be missed.

The same is true of still photography. However, photographs were found to be an invaluable mechanism for recording the experiences of the non-verbal child referred to in Chapter 4. Due to the slow pace of the communication aid, the researcher was able to take photos at particular stages of the learning walk, which later provided an invaluable stimulus for further reflection. Later this evidence was presented to her secondary school in preparation for her transition, which has been relatively smooth.

Interviews are usually a key element of data collection. As we have seen, there are many possible approaches to conducting interviews as part of a school-based inquiry (useful guidance on planning and carrying out interviews can be found in Powney and Watts, 1987). They may be guided by a set of pre-arranged questions that require almost predictable responses; on the other hand, they may take the form of a focused discussion around a set of prompting themes.

Interviews may take place with individuals, or in groups. Focus groups are an attractive method, especially when conducting research with children, not least because it is possible to include a larger group of participants. However, there is a danger, particularly with children, that the views of confident individuals may shape the contributions of others. The use of focus groups in the study described in Chapter 6 led to an additional opportunity for the children to interpret their own and each other's drawings – the stimulus of the other children's ideas shed further light on those drawings which had been difficult to interpret.

Beyond conventional observation and interview procedures, there is room for the use of more creative approaches in order to capture the views of others, particularly those of children. Shadowing groups of youngsters through a school day can provide adults with new and sometimes disturbing insights into what it is like to be a learner in a school. We recall, during such an exercise, learning about how some students go through the whole day in a secondary school without hearing an adult use their name. Such experiences remind us of the subtle ways in which some young people come to feel marginalised.

As illustrated in a number of the chapters, visual methods can be a particularly powerful way of engaging children. So, for example, drawings can be useful as a stimulus for individual or focus group interviews, or as the basis of the sorts of sociogram analysis described in Chapter 1. In a similar way, asking students to take photographs of different aspects of their school experience has proved to be particularly successful in enabling adults and other children to see school life through the eyes of the learner who has taken the photograph.

In India (in Chapter 5) it was the experience of speaking about the photos in front of a wider audience that had the greatest impact on a small group of learners with a range of disabilities whose views had never previously been sought. By contrast, in Chapter 9 photo-vignettes were created to depict some symptoms of a possible mental illness in order to stimulate discussion with young people in a secondary school and explore their attitudes.

The value of all of these forms of inquiry is, as we have suggested, that they 'make the familiar unfamiliar'. Commenting on this approach, Delamont (1992: 45) argues that familiarity can be a problem when doing applied research. With this in mind, she suggests devising strategies for 'making the familiar bizarre, unusual and novel', so that 'the familiarity is thus thrown into relief by the unfamiliar'.

It must be recognised, however, that such approaches have the potential to create disturbance. For example, Debra Martin (Chapter 3), as an insider practitioner and researcher, engaged in a new and, at times, disturbing process of collaborating with pupils to research their experience of becoming alienated from their local school. Such questions had not been asked before and the responses have interrupted thinking.

In our own research, we have worked with partner schools in order to explore ways of introducing a more critical dimension to the inquiry process. In particular, we have tried to find ways of encouraging practitioners to question their practices and, indeed, the assumptions behind these practices (Ainscow *et al.*, 2006). Through these approaches we seek to encourage discussions that are both supportive and yet challenging, and so stimulate self-questioning, creativity and action.

So, for example, we have seen how discussions of evidence have challenged existing assumptions as to the nature of educational difficulties experienced by some students. Specifically, we have observed how school staff begin to question the assumption that some students' characteristics are such that they require a different form of teaching from that offered to the majority of students. Such an orientation leads to a concern with finding the 'right' response, that is, different teaching methods or materials for pupils who do not respond to existing arrangements. Implicit in this formulation are the views that schools are rational organisations offering an appropriate range of opportunities; that those students who experience difficulties do so because of their own limitations or disadvantages; and that, therefore, they are in need of some form of special intervention (Skrtic, 1991). Our concern is that through such assumptions, leading to a search for effective responses to those children perceived as being 'different', opportunities for developments in practice may be overlooked.

The question for us, therefore, is why positive change occurs in some cases but not in others. Two sets of ideas are helpful in attempting to understand this question. These are Argyris and Schön's (1996) idea of single- and double-loop learning, referred to earlier, and Skrtic's (1991) distinction between bureaucracies and adhocracies, together with his notion of the recognition of 'anomalies' as the catalyst for the transition from one to the other.

Argyris and Schön (p. 72) describe the way that organisations 'learn' – to different extents and levels. *Single-loop learning* involves improvements to existing practice without any fundamental reconsideration of the assumptions on which that practice is based. *Double-loop learning* involves responding to questions about the underlying aims of practice and the implicit theories which underpin it.

Skrtic, who is specifically concerned with how schools respond to student diversity, also proposes a fundamental distinction in the way organisations solve problems. He argues that bureaucratic organisations deal with problems by creating different sub-units and specialisms to contain them, while practice elsewhere in the organisation remains undisturbed. However, what he defines as 'adhocratic' organisations see such problems as an opportunity to rethink their existing practices in fundamental ways. Skrtic argues that bureaucratic organisations can become adhocratic if enough of their members recognise 'anomalies' in existing practice.

In attempting to push thinking in these directions, we recognise that schools, like other social institutions, are influenced by perceptions of socio-economic status, race, language and gender. This being the case, we feel that it is essential to question how such perceptions influence classroom interactions.

Michele Moore's account of the difficulties faced by an urban primary school is rather worrying in this respect (Chapter 2). The school population is massively diverse and yet national policies appear to demand that the school offer a standardised response. The logical extension of this argument is that those youngsters who are seen as not meeting the standard are the problem.

At this stage we need to reiterate some of the key challenges in using inquiry-based approaches to school development. First of all, the intention is that it should be challenging to the thinking of everybody involved, not least those of us from universities who are involved in supporting colleagues in schools. Our assumptions are also challenged; we too have to find ways of dealing with and, hopefully, learning from one another's perspectives.

As with any form of research, a further challenge that needs to be addressed is that of trustworthiness: put simply, why should anybody take seriously the evidence that is collected? This is a particular issue in relation to forms of research that involve such a high degree of participation by stakeholders. Commenting on this, Schön (1991, p. 171) argues that without a serious effort to make clear what is meant by *rigour*, participatory research 'becomes an open sesame to woollyheadedness, a never-never land where anything goes'. He goes on to suggest that appropriate rigour in the study of practice should focus on validity (e.g. how do we know what we claim to know?) and utility (e.g. how useful is the research to practitioners?).

With this in mind, we recommend the use of triangulation, a technique that involves considering events from a number of viewpoints; for example: by comparing and contrasting evidence about the same actions and activities from different people (e.g. teachers, support staff and students); scrutinising events from different angles by making use of a variety of methods for collecting information; and using outsiders as observers. Most of the inquiries here have used a wide range of methods – a mosaic approach – to elicit children's views (Clark, 2004).

Another challenge is to analyse the multiplicity of data in a coherent and trustworthy manner. Our approach is to build levels of explanation and theorising by encouraging triangulation between different kinds of data and dialogue between different perspectives.

Influenced by the ideas of Karl Popper, Schön (1991) argues that the fundamental test for validity in participatory inquiry is through 'competitive resistance to refutation'. This involves juxtaposing alternate plausible accounts of the phenomenon in question. He notes: 'In the absence of an alternate hypothesis, one is likely to be overwhelmed by the obviousness of what one already knows' (348). With this advice in mind, we encourage practitioners to discuss the evidence collected through investigations in their schools, including alternative explanations as to what lessons could be drawn from these experiences.

Proposition 4: Strengthen collaboration

In order for it to be effective, an inquiry-based approach has to involve an element of challenge. It requires new thinking and, indeed, new relationships that promote active connections among practitioners and students, and stimulate risk taking and creative action. What, then, needs to be done to establish such conditions within a school community?

Where writers have addressed this agenda, they have tended to give particular emphasis to the characteristics of schools which stimulate and support processes of interrogation and reflection. For example, Skrtic (1991) argues that some schools are more likely to respond to student diversity in positive and creative ways. Such schools emphasise the pooling of different professional expertise in collaborative processes. They are also places where students who cannot easily be educated within established routines are not seen as 'having problems', but as challenging teachers to re-examine their practices in order to make them more responsive and flexible. The project described in Chapter 5, in which students with learning difficulties in a further education college became co-researchers with their support staff and tutor, is a striking example of collaborative processes leading to the re-examining of practice.

Our own research has pointed to organisational conditions – distributed leadership, high levels of staff and student involvement, joint planning, a commitment to inquiry and so on – that promote collaboration and problem-solving amongst staff, and which produce more inclusive responses to diversity (Ainscow, 1999). The efforts of the new head teacher referred to by Michele Moore (Chapter 2) to promote such an environment were met with hostility at first, but gradually changes were made possible, albeit more slowly than he would have liked.

Many of the forms of collaboration described in this book involved outsiders: a student researcher working with a class teacher and six 13–14-year-old boys in a school for children with social, emotional and behavioural difficulties (Chapter 11); a parent initiating an inquiry in the school in which her own disabled daughters are enrolled; a visiting behaviour specialist working with a class teacher and a group of five 6-year-olds (Chapter 7). Although the findings of these inquiries were illuminating and had an impact on a group of individuals, we have no evidence that suggests that they led to a wider culture of collaboration in these schools. This reminds us that the involvement of outsiders in strengthening collaboration through an inquiry process tends to be rather short-lived, and harder to sustain (as in India, Chapter 5) than those inquiries which are led by insiders.

How, then, can schools develop more inclusive cultures? As we explained in the Introduction, cultures are about basic assumptions and beliefs that are shared by members of an organisation, operating unconsciously to define how they view themselves and their working contexts. The extent to which these values include the acceptance and celebration of difference, and a commitment to all students, coupled with the extent to which they are shared across a school staff, are key factors in what we have described as an inclusive culture.

Changing the norms that exist within a school is difficult to achieve, particularly within a context where practitioners tend to work alone in addressing the problems they face (Rosenholtz, 1989). On the other hand, the presence of children who are not suited to the existing menu of the school can provide some encouragement to explore a more collaborative culture within which teachers support one another in experimenting with new teaching responses. So, to restate our argument, becoming more inclusive is a matter of thinking and talking, reviewing and refining practice, and making attempts to develop a more inclusive culture. Such a conceptualisation means that inclusion cannot be divorced from the contexts within which it is developing, nor the social relations that might sustain or limit that development.

Following similar lines, other researchers argue that in order to bring about the cultural change that inclusion demands, it is essential to consider the values underlying the intended changes (Corbett 2001; Carrington 1999; Kugelmass 2001). Thus, cultural change is directed towards a 'transformative view of inclusion, in which diversity is seen as making a positive contribution to the creation of responsive educational settings' (Ainscow *et al.*, 2006: 15).

Proposition 5: Adopt forms of leadership that encourage a spirit of enquiry

In reflecting on the process of compiling the accounts presented in this book, we are conscious that a small number of inspired and inspiring head teachers enabled our students to carry out inquiries in their busy school environments. Not only did they enable this process to take place, but they actively encouraged student participation and frequently attended meetings at the university to discuss and contribute to the process. They realised, too, that this was a risky process, but they seemed to welcome the challenge and saw it as a learning opportunity. In fact, they frequently commented on how useful the meetings were in providing a unique insight into their colleagues' practice.

These experiences offer further support to our belief that the development of more inclusive approaches does not arise from a mechanical process in which any one specific organisational restructuring, or the introduction of a particular set of techniques, generates increased levels of participation. Rather, as we have argued, the development of inclusive practices requires processes of social learning within particular organisational contexts. As classrooms continue to become more diverse, schools will need to develop this increased capacity for collective problem-solving in order to respond appropriately to a wider range of learners. This, in turn, points to the importance of leadership in order to make this happen.

It is encouraging, therefore, that recent research on educational leadership has paid increasing attention to this theme (Ainscow and Sandill, 2010). So, for example, as a result of their extensive literature review, Leithwood and Riehl (2005) contend that developing people by providing intellectual stimulation is one of the core practices of effective leadership. Lambert and her colleagues seem to be talking about a similar approach when they stress the importance of leaders gathering, generating and interpreting information within a school in order to create an 'inquiring stance'. They argue that such information causes 'disequilibrium' in thinking and, as a result, provides a challenge to existing assumptions about teaching and learning (Lambert *et al.*, 1995). We have called this *making interruptions* and, in so doing, stressed the importance of social relations within a school as a factor in making them productive.

Much of the literature on the role of leadership in relation to school improvement places emphasis on the importance of social relationships (e.g. Fullan, 1991; Hopkins *et al.*, 1994; Hopkins, 2008). Johnson and Johnson (1989), two key figures in the field of social psychology, argue that leaders may structure staff working relationships in one of three ways: competitively, individualistically or cooperatively. Within a competitive structure, teachers work against each other to achieve a goal that only a few can attain; an individualistic structure exists when teachers work alone to accomplish goals that are unrelated to the goals of their colleagues; and a cooperative structure exists when teachers coordinate their efforts to achieve joint goals. They go on to argue that to maximise the productivity of a school, principals have to: challenge the status quo of traditional competitive and individualistic approaches to teaching; inspire a clear mutual vision of what the school should and could be; empower staff through cooperative teamwork; lead by example, using cooperative procedures and taking risks; and encourage staff members to persist and keep striving to improve their expertise. Within this overall formulation, the authors place a strong emphasis on the need to build cooperative teams within which there is a strong sense of inter-dependence amongst team members.

In a way that sums up the implications for leadership, following another review of research literature, Riehl (2000) suggests that school leaders need to attend to three broad types of task: fostering new meanings about diversity; promoting inclusive practices within schools; and building connections between schools and communities. She goes on to consider how these tasks can be accomplished, exploring how the concept of practice, especially discursive practice, can contribute to a fuller understanding of the work of school principals. This analysis leads her to offer a positive view of the potential for school principals to engage in inclusive, transformative developments. She concludes: 'When wedded to a relentless commitment to equity, voice, and social justice, administrators' efforts in the tasks of sense-making, promoting inclusive cultures and practices in schools, and building positive relationships outside of the school may indeed foster a new form of practice' (71).

Looking to the future: equity in education

We have outlined five working propositions that have emerged from our research with schools that can help those who wish to use an inquiry-based approach in developing a greater capacity for responding to learner diversity. Essentially, we are advocating that inquiries should start where schools are, by: making use of existing expertise; creating conversations about practice; using evidence as the catalyst for change; strengthening collaboration; and finally, but perhaps most importantly, adopting forms of leadership that encourage a spirit of inquiry.

The accounts we have presented provide interesting insights into the difficulties facing those who attempt to use such an approach and how these can be addressed. Our reading of these accounts leads us to conclude that significant advances in schooling, and education more broadly, are unlikely to be achieved unless those who remain on the margins of the system are transformed into full and equal participants. In other words, we need policies and practices that will encourage equity, which we take to mean both inclusion (*being there*) and fairness (*being treated equally*).

The ideas developed in the book are particularly timely as national policies in the UK place increased emphasis on finding ways of 'closing the gap' between high- and low-performing learners, and in so doing, break the link between disadvantaged home backgrounds and educational outcomes. The government has argued that efforts to 'raise standards' must also promote equity: that a powerful emphasis on improving attainment need not simply benefit children who are already performing at a high level. Implemented properly, and supported by the various inclusion initiatives, the standards agenda is, it is argued, of even greater potential benefit to previously low-attaining students: it is about excellence for the many, not just the few.

Yet, the various national strategies that have been used to achieve this goal, whatever their benefits, have tended to reduce the flexibility with which schools can respond to the diverse characteristics of their students. At the same time, the development of an educational marketplace, coupled with the recent emphasis on policies fostering greater diversity between schools, seem to have created a quasi-selective system in which the poorest children, by and large, attend the lowest-performing schools. Consequently, the lowest-performing and, many would argue, the least advantaged schools, fall progressively further and further behind their high-performing counterparts (Ainscow *et al.*, 2009).

In terms of these effects, through selective advantaging and disadvantaging of schools, it can be argued that those very policies that have generally led to increased standards, have also increased, rather than decreased, disparities in education quality and opportunity between advantaged and less privileged groups. Giroux and Schmidt (2004) explain how similar reform policies in the USA have turned some schools into 'test-prep centres'. As a result, such schools tend to be increasingly ruthless in their disregard of those students who pose a threat to their 'success', as determined by standardised, but narrow, assessment procedures.

Nevertheless, our analysis of the experiences described in this book offers some reasons for optimism, not least in that it supports our view that the system has considerable untapped potential to improve itself. As we have seen, there are skills, knowledge and, most importantly, creativity within schools, and within their local communities, that can be mobilised to improve provision for learner diversity.

All of this demonstrates what can be achieved when those who have a stake in education engage in authentic collaborative activity. Of course, collaboration has itself been a regular feature of national policy in recent years, best illustrated by initiatives such as Excellence in Cities, the Leadership Incentive Grant and City Challenge. Nevertheless, and despite this press for greater collaboration within and between schools, there has been a tendency to view schools through a deficit lens, focusing on what they lack rather than the resources upon which they can draw. As a result, it has often been assumed that externally driven strategies are the only feasible means of achieving improvement.

Our own commitment to the potential of collaborative action research as a means of using insider knowledge to drive improvement efforts has been influenced by our involvement in projects of the sort reported in this book. It has also been shaped by the work of many others, not least the ideas of Wenger (1998), Senge (1992) and Hargreaves (2003).

In putting forward his notion of 'communities of practice', Wenger (1998) describes the transfer and creation of knowledge within the workplace. Essentially, the members of a work community pass on their knowledge and ideas to one another through processes of 'negotiation' in which common meanings are established. 'New' knowledge acquired in this way can then be tested out in practice – though inevitably it will be modified as it is subjected to new experiences and contexts. As it moves around, passing from practitioner to practitioner, knowledge is continually modified and refined. In this way, it becomes possible for knowledge to be recycled around the community and returned to the originator – though transformed through the process.

Thus, the virtuous circle is completed, with knowledge and understanding increased through each iteration.

In his writings on what he calls 'learning organisations', Senge (1992) suggests that knowledge within organisations takes two forms – the explicit and the tacit. Explicit knowledge (which will embrace established wisdom) is relatively easy to transfer, but is likely to be generalised rather than specific. On the other hand, tacit knowledge is caught rather than deliberately passed on, but can only be caught if the right circumstances exist. Consequently, what can be achieved through explicit and tacit exchanges is limited – learning organisations need to find ways to generate tacit-to-explicit and explicit-to-tacit transfers. Again, our conception of collaborative practice is that it provides just such an opportunity, as individuals work together on common goals, sharing and using one another's knowledge and, through the processes of sharing, reflection and recycling, create new knowledge.

Hargreaves (2003) also notes the tacit nature of much of teachers' knowledge when explaining why it has proved so difficult to transfer good practice from one teacher to another. This leads him to conclude that what he describes as 'social capital' is needed within teaching communities. *Social capital* here represents shared values and assumptions that, because they are commonly 'owned' by community members, are available for all members of the community to draw on when transferring knowledge and understandings. For him, building social capital involves the development of networks based on mutual trust, within which good practice can spread in natural ways.

Bearing these ideas in mind, we conclude that collaboration within schools, stimulated and challenged by an engagement with evidence – and with the support of advisers, where appropriate – is a practice that can both transfer existing knowledge and, more importantly, generate context-specific new knowledge. In this way, learner differences no longer pose a problem to be solved or removed; rather they become the necessary resource that can stimulate the sorts of working relationships, creativity and responsive approaches to teaching that are needed in order to produce an education system that is genuinely equitable. The studies reported in this book give strong indications of how such processes can be initiated and managed.

References

Ainscow, M. (1999) *Understanding the Development of Inclusive Schools*. London: Falmer.

Ainscow, M. and Kaplan, I. (2005) 'Using evidence to encourage inclusive school development: possibilities and challenges'. *Australasian Journal of Special Education* 29(2): 106–116.

Ainscow, M. and Sandill, A. (2010) 'Developing inclusive education systems: the role of organisational cultures and leadership'. *International Journal of Inclusive Education* in press.

Ainscow, M., Booth, T., Dyson, A., with Farrell, P., Frankham, J., Gallannaugh, F., Howes, A. and Smith, R. (2006) *Improving Schools, Developing Inclusion.* London: Routledge.

Ainscow, M., Conteh, J., Dyson, A. and Gallannaugh, F. (2007) *Children in Primary Education: Demography, Culture, Identity, Diversity, Inclusion (Research Survey 5:1).* Cambridge: University of Cambridge.

Ainscow, M., Dyson, A., Goldrick, S. and Kerr, K. (2009) 'Using research to foster inclusion and equity within the context of New Labour education reforms'. In C. Chapman and H. Gunter (eds) *Radical Reforms: Perspectives on an Era of Educational Change.* London: Routledge, pp. 169–181.

Argyris, C. and Schön, D. A. (1996) *Organizational Learning II: Theory, Method and Practice.* Reading, MA: Addison-Wesley.

Armstrong, F. and Moore, M. (eds) (2004) *Action Research for Inclusive Education.* London: Routledge.

Artiles, A. J. and Dyson, A. (2005) 'Inclusive education in the globalization age: the promise of comparative cultural-historical analysis'. In D. Mitchell (ed.) *Contextualizing Inclusive Education: Evaluating Old and New International Perspectives.* London: Routledge, pp. 37–62.

Booth, T. and Ainscow, M. (2002) *The Index for Inclusion* (2nd edn). Bristol: Centre for Studies on Inclusive Education.

Carrington, S. (1999) 'Inclusion needs a different school culture'. *International Journal of Inclusive Education* 3(3): 257–268.

Clark, A. (2004) 'The mosaic approach and research with young children'. In V. Lewis, M. Kellett, C. Robinson, S. Fraser and S. Ding *The Reality of Research with Children and Young People.* London: Sage, pp. 142–162.

Corbett, J. (2001) *Supporting Inclusive Education: A Connective Pedagogy.* London: Routledge.

Delamont, S. (1992) *Fieldwork in Educational Settings: Methods, Pitfalls and Perspectives.* London: Falmer.

Dyson, A. (2006) 'Beyond the school gates: context, disadvantage and "urban schools"'. In M. Ainscow and M. West (eds) *Improving Urban Schools: Leadership and Collaboration.* Maidenhead: Open University Press.

Elliott, J. (1991) *Action Research for Educational Change.* Buckingham: Open University Press.

Fielding, M. (2001) 'Students as radical agents of change'. *Journal of Educational Change* 2(2): 123–141.

Fullan, M. (1991) *The New Meaning of Educational Change.* London: Cassell.

Giroux, H. A. and Schmidt, M. (2004) 'Closing the achievement gap: a metaphor for children left behind'. *Journal of Educational Change* 5: 213–228.

Hammersley, M. (1992) *What's Wrong with Ethnography?* London: Routledge.

Hargreaves, D. H. (2003) *Education Epidemic: Transforming Secondary Schools Through Innovation Networks.* London: Demos.

Hopkins, D. (2008) *A Teacher's Guide to Classroom Research* (4th edn). Maidenhead: Open University Press.

Hopkins, D., Ainscow, M. and West, M. (1994) *School Improvement in an Era of Change.* London: Cassell.

Howes, A. and Ainscow, M. (2006) 'Collaboration with a city-wide purpose: making paths for sustainable educational improvement'. In M. Ainscow and M. West (eds)

Improving Urban Schools: Leadership and Collaboration. Maidenhead: Open University Press.

Iano, R. P. (1986) 'The study and development of teaching: with implications for the advancement of special education'. *Remedial and Special Education* 7(5): 50–61.

Johnson, D. W. and Johnson, R. (1989) *Learning Together and Alone: Cooperative, Competitive, and Individualistic Learning*. Boston: Allyn & Bacon.

Kugelmass, J. (2001) 'Collaboration and compromise in creating and sustaining an inclusive school'. *International Journal of Inclusive Education* 5(1): 47–65

Lambert, L., Walker, D., Zimmerman, D. P., Cooper, J. E., Lampert, M. D., Gardner, M. E. and Szabo, M. (1995) *The Constructivist Leader*. New York: Teachers College Press.

Leithwood, K. A. and Riehl, C. J. (2005) 'What do we already know about educational leadership?' In W. A. Firestone (ed.) *A New Agenda for Research in Educational Leadership*. New York: Teachers College Press, pp. 12–27.

Lewin, K. (1946) 'Action research and minority problems'. *Journal of Social Issues* 2(4): 34–36.

O'Hanlon, C. (2003) *Educational Inclusion as Action Research*. Maidenhead: Open University Press.

Poplin, M. and Weeres, J. (1992) *Voices from the Inside: A Report on Schooling from Inside the Classroom*. Claremont, CA: Institute for Education in Transformation.

Powney, J. and Watts, M. (1987) *Interviewing in Educational Research*. London: Routledge.

Riehl, C. J. (2000) 'The principal's role in creating inclusive schools for diverse students: a review of normative, empirical, and critical literature on the practice of educational administration'. *Review of Educational Research* 70(1): 55–81.

Robinson, V. M. J. (1998) 'Methodology and the research-practice gap'. *Educational Researcher* 27: 17–26.

Robson, C. (2002) *Real World Research* (2nd edn). London: Blackwell Publishing.

Rosenholtz, S. (1989) *Teachers' Workplace: The Social Organisation of Schools*. New York: Longman.

Schön, D. (ed.) (1991) *The Reflective Turn*. New York: Teachers College Press.

Senge, P. M. (1992) *The Fifth Discipline*. London: Century Business.

Skrtic, T. (1991) *Behind Special Education: A Critical Analysis of Professional Culture and School Organization*. Denver: Love.

Stubbs, S. (1995) *The Lesotho National Integrated Education Programme: A Case Study on Implementation*. Unpublished M.Ed thesis, Faculty of Education, University of Cambridge.

Trent, S. C., Artiles, A.J. and Englert, C. S. (1998) 'From deficit thinking to social constructivism: a review of theory, research and practice in special education'. *Review of Research in Education* 23: 277–307

Wenger, E. (1998) *Communities of Practice: Learning, Meaning and Identity*. Cambridge: Cambridge University Press.

Winter, R. (1989) *Learning from Experience: Principles and Practice in Action Research*. London: Falmer.

Appendix: 'School-based inquiry and development'

An innovative approach to professional learning

The Master's level course unit referred to in this book has been developed over the last 15 years in the School of Education, University of Manchester. Inspired by what is known in the University's Business School as the 'Manchester Method' (Rickards and Moger, 1996), in this short summary of the course, we aim to share with readers the philosophy underpinning the curriculum content, as well as the practical considerations involved in guiding groups of students through a collaborative inquiry in the real world setting of a school.

An organisational approach to inclusion and diversity

Students come from all over the world to study in Manchester, and they bring with them their own culturally and contextually determined concepts of education, inclusive education, diversity and pedagogy. For the majority, inclusive education is strongly associated with the 'special educational needs' of individual children, rather than the way in which the education system is organised to respond to the needs of various groups of children. Yet, the concept of inclusive education is not fixed; rather it is a process which is constantly evolving, and is determined by context.

The main aim of postgraduate study in this contested field is to prepare students to evaluate current developments, both in the UK and internationally, in relation to their own present and future practice. The diverse nature of the student group is both a tremendous strength and a considerable challenge – this is felt most strongly in the course unit, 'School-based inquiry and development'. The students have found this course unit the most challenging – logistically, personally and intellectually. It has been a steep, and sometimes painful, learning curve for all involved. Yet, the learning that has taken place has been profound, and sometimes life-changing.

In addition to school-based methods of research and inquiry, topics covered in lectures include: urban education; management of change; action research approaches; observation skills; using innovative methods; working collaboratively; keeping a research diary; making sense of evidence; and evaluating the impact of innovation.

A personalised and a collaborative approach to learning

Students are expected to learn both collaboratively with their peers and independently. Assignment titles are negotiated between tutors and individual students to ensure that the course of study is tailored to their own individual research interests.

The 'School-based inquiry and development' course enables full-time and part-time students to conduct a small-scale collaborative study either in a local school arranged by university staff, or in their place of work. Relationships have been developed between university staff and nearby schools, largely through university-led research projects. As head teachers have come to appreciate the value of having a team of researchers conducting an inquiry, the word has spread and students' presence in schools has come to be seen as an asset. Four students, who each spend 10 days in a school, contribute 40 working days in research time – this is a major contribution to the process of school self-evaluation and is seen positively by inspectors.

Working in teams of three to four, students are expected to design and conduct a small-scale inquiry in collaboration with key members of school staff. In the case of students who are already employed as a member of staff in an educational setting, they would be encouraged to develop a research partnership with colleagues or students in that setting.

Within a very short time students are exposed to some of the complexities involved in inquiring into inclusive practices in schools with diverse populations, situated in communities facing considerable economic deprivation. For those who are already working in such contexts, they begin to see their familiar surroundings in new and unfamiliar ways. This is not always a comfortable process – rather, it can cause a great deal of disturbance within the researcher and within the team.

Logistics

The student groups are determined by the course leader, in consultation with students, based on minimal knowledge of their abilities, backgrounds and personalities. Extra care is taken to ensure a balance of cultural backgrounds, languages spoken and computer skills. The groups are diverse – usually each member of a research team comes from a different cultural background and educational tradition. One group, for example, included students from

India, Zimbabwe, Nigeria and the Netherlands – representing three different continents! Another group included students from Greece, the USA and Zimbabwe. Schools have sometimes requested students of Chinese or Pakistani heritage, as they can provide positive role models for their students while conducting the inquiry.

Schools are encouraged to identify a person, or even a team of people, to take responsibility for working with the students on the research task. It is the responsibility of the school team to work with colleagues to identify a problem, an issue of concern or a question they would like to address. Initially, we had a link person employed by the Manchester City Council (Michele Moore) who helped the schools to think through the 'problem' they identified, and so act as the 'problem-broker'. Now this role is played by the course leader, as appropriate.

It is the responsibility of each group to arrange a preliminary meeting at the school – their first collaborative task! The students complete their initial fact-finding visits to the schools, and discuss the 'research task' with relevant members of staff. It is at this point that they begin to formulate their research questions, based on the problem identified by the school.

A central part of the inquiry process is the keeping of a research diary. One part of the formal assessment is a piece of self-critical reflective writing which analyses the school context and makes an assessment of the research task using excerpts from the diary as evidence. This assignment also involves an assessment of the challenges involved in conducting a *collaborative* inquiry. It is often striking how very different these accounts are, and how differently the individual members perceive the collaborative task.

Formal presentations of the findings are made by each research team as part of their assessment. The presentations include: the problem they faced; the research plan; research methods used; findings and recommendations; and reflections on the difficulties encountered and lessons learnt. The final part of the assignment is a report, written collaboratively by the research team, which outlines the problem, the research process and the limitations of the research, and ethical issues and recommendations.

Following the formal assessment process for the M.Ed programme, all schools are offered the opportunity of a formal presentation by students in a staff meeting, and short summary reports (two to three pages) are prepared for the schools. Some schools request the full reports, which are on average 20 pages in length. Some of the short reports have been incorporated into school development plans and have been much admired during Ofsted inspections.

Reference

Rickards, T. and Moger, S. (1996) Editorial. *Creativity and Innovation Management* 5(1): 1–2.

Index